The Work-at-Home Success Bible

A Complete Guide for Women

Leslie Truex

BUSINESS

Avon, Massachusetts

DEDICATION

To all women who are looking to create
fulfilling careers and have inspired lives.

Published by
Adams Business, an imprint of Adams Media, a division of F+W Media, Inc.
57 Littlefield Street, Avon, MA 02322. U.S.A.
www.adamsmedia.com

ISBN 10: 1-59869-916-4
ISBN 13: 978-1-59869-916-6

Printed in the United States of America.

J I H G F E D C B A

Library of Congress Cataloging-in-Publication Data
is available from the publisher.

This publication is designed to provide accurate and authoritative information
with regard to the subject matter covered. It is sold with the understanding that
the publisher is not engaged in rendering legal, accounting, or other professional
advice. If legal advice or other expert assistance is required, the services of a competent professional person should be sought.
—From a *Declaration of Principles* jointly adopted by a Committee of the
American Bar Association and a Committee of Publishers and Associations

Many of the designations used by manufacturers and sellers to distinguish their
product are claimed as trademarks. Where those designations appear in this book
and Adams Media was aware of a trademark claim, the designations have been
printed with initial capital letters.

This book is available at quantity discounts for bulk purchases.
For information, please call 1-800-289-0963.

Contents

Acknowledgments

Wow. Where do I start in thanking everyone who has had a hand in making this project possible? First I want to thank my parents, all four of them, for their support and assistance. Thank you to my children, Zachary and Hannah, who were the inspiration behind my wanting to work at home and continue as my cheerleaders as I embark on new projects. I want to give a very special thanks to my husband Jay, who has always supported me, even when I was flailing and failing in my effort to work at home.

Thank you to all the WorkAtHomeSuccess.com readers, and my online friends and mentors for all your support, advice, and friendship! Thanks also to Jennifer Zajac, Nell Taliercio, Heidi Marshall, Jenn Cangelosi, Kitara R. Wilson, Angela Wills, Annette Yen, Adriana Copaceanu, and Tammy Kipf for sharing their success stories.

Finally, a big thank you to Lilly Ghahremani and Stephanie Von Borstel, agents extraordinaire, for taking a chance with a forty-something pajama-clad work-at-home mom, and especially to Lilly for helping me find my voice. And thank you to Peter Archer, my editor at Adams Media, for being so approachable and helpful to this novice author.

Introduction

As I watch my children waiting for the bus through the front window of my home, I can't help but notice all the cars passing by carrying some poor soul clad in a red power noose (aka, a tie) or sausage casings (known as pantyhose) on the way to a job. They have glazed looks in their eyes despite the travel mug of hot coffee sitting in their cup holder. "Why do they do it?" I wonder. Then the bus comes, I grab my coffee mug, and head down the hall to my office dressed in my pajamas and fuzzy slippers. I power on my laptop, turn on iTunes, and go to work. Ah, the life of a pajama mama!

You picked up this book because you want to join the ranks of comfortably clad women who set their own hours and work from the comfort of their own homes. The good news is that you can. Millions of women just like you have already taken advantage of the increasing number of employers offering work-at-home options. Other women have seized control of their careers, leaving the rat race to start a home business that has afforded them the flexibility and financial stability that jobs have failed to provide. The work-at-home trend is expected to continue giving you more and more opportunities to join us.

What Qualifies Me to Be Your Coach?

Why should you take advice from a forty-something mom who spends most of her day in her pajamas? Because I've been where you are and I'm now where you'd like to be. I struggled to find my way through the work-at-home jungle of scams and crazy schemes, until I found success. I've telecommuted online and off as a social worker, writer, and researcher. I've started a variety of home businesses, some that failed, and some that made money. Through study, research, and lots of action, I was able to create a work-at-home career that I love. Today, I telecommute part time as an adoption social worker, run a successful website that earns income through advertising and affiliate programs, and create information products related to working at home. You're holding one of those products right now.

However, it didn't happen overnight. One thing I hate about infomercials and many how-to gurus is how they give the impression that your life can change today with very little effort and $49.99 plus shipping and handling. My journey to work-at-home success was not fast or easy. It was a lot of work. I had setbacks and disappointments. I failed, several times. But I was determined to create a life that gave me the income I needed while still being able to be at home with my children and pursue personal interests. Today I live that life, and I want to help you do the same!

What You'll Get from This Book

The Work-at-Home Success Bible will show you the real deal about working at home. You'll discover why telecommuting is growing, what companies want in home-based employees, and how you can take advantage of it. You'll also learn about home business and how you can turn your hobby or passion into a home-based career you love, as well as get paid what you're worth (finally!). Further, you'll learn how you can telecommute or start a home business (or both) using the Internet.

But more than a book filled with information, *The Work-at-Home Success Bible* will take you step by step through creating a plan of action so that starting today, you'll be taking steps to work at home. When you finish the book, you'll have a work-at-home proposal to show your boss, or a winning resume to apply for a work-at-home job. Or maybe you'll have a business plan in place and be ready to take your first customer.

What This Book Can't Do

Like a recipe, this guide tells you exactly what to do to cook up the career of your dreams. But for it to work, you need to do the activities provided in the book. You can read a book about baking a pie, but you won't have dessert unless you put the ingredients in the bowl, mix them up, and cook them. The same is true of working at home: It takes action.

I don't know about you, but I frequently skip over exercises and worksheets in books, usually because I can't see how they are going to help me learn what I want to know. You won't have that problem here, as the exercises are directly related to helping you find or create a work-at-home job or business.

Plan for Work-at-Home Success

How long have you been thinking of working at home? A week? Six months? Three years? Longer? Thinking about what you want in life is a good first step, but thinking by itself doesn't get things done. I think about investing in real estate and writing a mystery novel. But I own only one home (the one I live in) and I don't have a book in the mystery section of the bookstore.

To be successful at working at home, or anything else, requires action. By reading this book and doing the activities, you're taking action. But when this book is done, you'll still have more steps to take, whether it's talking to your boss, applying for a new job, or getting a business permit. The best way to ensure that thoughts are followed by action is to have a plan. Research suggests that writing your plan will increase the chances of your following through, so throughout this book, you'll be creating your plan based on the work-at-home options you choose. The sections marked "Plan for Work-at-Home Success" will be your cue to take action. While you can write in this book, I recommend that you get a notebook where you can keep all your information organized in one place.

All the resources and information are correct at the time of this writing, but things can change, particularly online. You can find up-to-date information and resources as well as copies of the worksheets found in this book by visiting the Work-at-Home Success website at *www.workathomesuccess.com*.

If you're ready to discover all the ways you can work at home and set a course to make it happen, throw on your pajamas and let's get started . . .

Part One

LIVING AND WORKING AT HOME

CHAPTER ONE
The Reality of Living and Working at Home

WHEN I FIRST WANTED TO WORK AT HOME, I had a vision of how perfect my life would be. I'd sleep in or nap during the day, or both! I'd feed my kids hot breakfasts and volunteer at their school. Then I'd take them to the park and on long walks. I'd work out at the gym every day. And my house would be spotless. What a life it would be!

But did you notice something I wasn't doing? Working. When I imagined working at home, I rarely imagined the work part. But there is work. And except for the sleeping in and napping, just about all I imagined hasn't come true. My kids have cold cereal they fix themselves for breakfast. My home is a disaster, and while I run a few days a week, I'm not a hot gym mama.

The reality of working at home is very different from what most people imagine, so it's important to consider all the advantages and disadvantages before embarking on your work-at-home career.

Advantages to Working at Home

- *Control your time:* While not true in all cases, working at home can usually give you the flexibility to work the hours you choose.

- *Earn what you're worth:* According to the National Committee on Pay Equity, women still earn only about seventy-seven cents for each dollar a man earns for the same work. The only way to remedy this is to create your own job and set your own salary.

- *Create the ideal career:* Imagine doing a job that excites you and nourishes your spirit. Working at home lets you create a career that can do just that.

- *Never a dull moment:* Although not all the excitement is the "Woo-Hoo" type, you can be sure that you'll hardly ever be bored.

- *Challenge your mind:* No more walking on the career treadmill doing the same things day after day. Working at home challenges your mind to be creative, solve problems, and think quickly.

Disadvantages to Working at Home

- *Longer work hours:* It's possible, particularly in the early days of your work-at-home career, that you'll work more, not less.

- *No set payday:* In most work-at-home situations, even in telecommuting, you only get paid when you work, resulting in irregular paydays.

- *Develop a dislike for your passion:* If you turn your hobby or passion into your job, you may learn to hate it when it becomes something you have to do.

■ *Stressful:* Irregular paydays and checks, looming dead-lines, multiple projects, along with all of life's other challenges, can become stressful.

■ *It's all on you:* Particularly in a home business, your success, your income, everything rides on you.

■ *Mental energy drain:* Even when you aren't working, you're thinking about your job or business. This can sap your energy and make you feel like you're working 24/7 even when you're only working two hours a day.

■ *Isolation:* Working at home is a lonely sport. It's ideal for getting lots done, but you'll miss out on office gossip and stimulating conversation.

Have I scared you yet? No? Good. Because the advantages of working at home far outweigh the disadvantages.

What Working at Home Won't Be Like

I discovered the hard way that working at home is not that much different from working in a traditional job or business, except of course I don't have to wear high heels. When I first decided to work at home, I got caught up in all the ads and offers that indicated I could stuff envelopes, type, read, surf the web, and track refunds. I'm not alone. Too many women conduct their work-at-home search looking for the wrong types of work in the wrong places. So I want to set you on the right path by sharing with you what working is really about.

When you work at home you won't be a:

■ Typist (although you may be a transcriptionist)
■ Envelope stuffer
■ Assembly crafter
■ Data entry specialist

- E-mail processor
- Rebate processor
- Transaction processor
- Refund tracer
- Ad placer
- Web surfer
- Survey taker (Although surveys are fun and can result in fun prizes, it won't pay the rent.)
- Member who signs up and does nothing (This may seem obvious, but I find work-at-home offers all the time that suggest you can make millions just by signing up.)

Instead, people who work at home do real types of work like writing, customer service, sales, research, web design, graphic design, virtual assistance, social work, nursing, teaching . . . the list goes on and on. When it comes to working at home you won't simply sign up and make money; instead, you'll apply for a real job or start a real business, and work hard to make it a success.

Working at home can be better and more fun than commuting to a job, but it's not necessarily easier. You may not have more time and your house probably won't be cleaner. You'll have frustrations and disappointments along the way. Life won't become a cruise on which you catch and ride a wave. There will be times in which there is no wind and you'll have to create your own energy to get moving. Other times there will be storms and you'll be holding on tight to keep from sinking.

I'm not saying this to scare you, but to prepare you. Too many people have the idea that working at home is simple . . . 1) Sign up, 2) Work, 3) Get paid, 4) Play the rest of the day. Its just not like that, and you need to have the mindset that recognizes that it will be work, sometimes easy and sometimes hard, even seemingly impossible.

Fortunately, this book will give you the knowledge and tools you need to navigate the road to work-at-home success.

LAW OF WORK-AT-HOME SUCCESS #❶
You can't simply sign up to make money at home.

What It Takes to Succeed at Home

There are no guarantees when it comes to working at home. To improve your chances of success, you need the skills, mindset, and attitude that lead to success, including:

A do-what-it-takes attitude. People frequently ask me, "What is the best work-at-home opportunity?" The answer is, "The one you'll do." Success in working at home isn't about the opportunity you choose, it's about whether or not you do it. If you don't do the work, you don't get paid, you don't work at home.

A burning desire to succeed. There is a saying in network marketing circles that goes something like, "When you have a big enough 'why,' the how will come." Essentially, if your desire is great enough, you'll figure out how to reach your goal. This is true in working at home. Your desire will be the fuel that powers you over the bumps in the road to work-at-home success.

Confidence. Henry Ford is quoted as saying, "If you think you can or you can't, you're right." When it comes to working at home, it helps to have confidence in your talents and a belief that you can do it.

A willingness to take risks. You don't have to be the type of person who bungee jumps off a bridge or goes into debt for the "sure thing," but there are calculated risks associated with working at home.

A commitment to yourself and your endeavor. Working at home is like having a baby. Babies are wonderful, beautiful creatures. But they cry a lot. They need constant attention and they require an enormous amount of patience. Your work-at-home endeavor will be the same. But just like you can't give up the baby, you can't give up on working at home. You have to nurture it, be patient, try new approaches, and no matter what, never quit.

Self-discipline. While working at home allows for some flexibility, you need to be diligent about working. It is amazingly easy to spend the day eating, doing laundry, and running errands, and not getting a single piece of work done. I know because that's all I did the first week I was home full time.

Staying focused. Being clear about your work duties is one thing, ignoring the laundry, TV, and refrigerator is another. Then there is the Internet, e-mail, instant messaging, games, YouTube . . . etc. If necessary, you need to hide your work area from distractions either by closing a door or having the ability to ignore everything but your work. And you need to be diligent about working instead of playing while online. (A FireFox web browser add-on called LeechBlock can be used to block time-wasting URLs during times of the day you specify. If you use FireFox, visit *https://addons.mozilla.org/en-US/firefox/ addon/4476* for details.)

Flexibility. There may be times in which you'll need to meet a client or boss on short notice. Switching gears is an enormously helpful talent when life happens and gets in the way of scheduled plans.

Motivation. Part of being motivated is maintaining your "why"—that compelling, action-driving reason that keeps you working when you'd rather nap or quit. But it also includes understanding and taking advantage of your peak work hours and conditions. Further, you need strategies to keep motivated when your energy is low, such as energetic or inspiring music or a goal to work toward.

Being prepared. Working at home requires anticipating your needs and organizing your tasks and supplies to make optimum use of your time and energy.

Accountability to yourself and others. Just because you have the option to work at home doesn't mean you're not part of a larger group that relies on you to do your part. Meeting deadlines and completing tasks will be essential to your success.

Decisiveness. When "stuff" happens, and it will, you won't have someone in the next cubicle to help you make decisions. You're on your own in analyzing, problem-solving, and fixing issues that arise.

Resourcefulness. Women are naturally resourceful. They have invented some of the greatest gadgets of the last decade, such as salad scissors and hair towels that aren't bulky, but still absorb water. Working at home requires much of that same kind of resourcefulness toward solving problems. You need to know where to get help or find information, and then figure out how to make things work when there are no obvious solutions.

Organization. Work-at-home jobs and businesses tend to be task or project oriented. Without good organization, you can waste time wading through lists and information without accomplishing any work. Developing a method of staying on task and keeping necessary materials and information within easy reach is crucial to using your time efficiently.

Outside-the-Box Thinking. With limited resources, creativity can go a long way to solving problems.

Diplomacy. There will be people who complain. Sometimes they'll complain about things you have no control over. Regardless of the situation, you need to be calm and professional when dealing with people.

Discretion. You may be working at home by yourself, but the information and resources (and even secrets) you deal with will involve other people. Protect your client's or employer's information and keep details about their lives or businesses in confidence.

If you don't feel you have all these traits, don't worry. Many can be developed or overcome. On the other hand, there are some traits that you'll absolutely need to have to succeed, including a good work ethic, resourcefulness, and flexibility. If you prefer a work environment with a strict routine and lots of external cues (e.g., cubicles and meetings), then working at home may not be for you. If you don't like carrying the sole burden of work or fluctuating income, then it may not be for you either. But if you're willing to put in the time and develop the skills you need, then there is no reason why you won't succeed at home.

Having the Time of Your Life

Have you ever heard anyone complain about having too much time on their hands? Me either. We're all busy. We have jobs, kids, relatives, commitments, bills, housework, repairs, and reality TV to deal with. So how are you going to fit your work-at-home action plan into an already packed schedule?

I once read an article that said "busy people get more done." That seems obvious, but the point was that when people had extra time, they didn't make good use of it. I coached a young mother who had a five-year-old son that she wanted to home school and a part time job she wasn't thrilled about. She was very active in her business, attending teleconferences for training, running ads and marketing online, all while working a part-time job and being a wife and mother. Within a few months (about the time school was to start), she and her husband determined that she could quit her part time job and stay home. But once she quit her job, she couldn't find the time to build her business, despite the fact that she had at least twenty more hours of time a week. Even though she had more time, for some reason she ran out of time to work on her business.

So what happens to that time? Many women feel guilty in pursuing their own interests and dreams, so activities related to working at home get pushed behind everything else. What I find most fascinating is that most women who want to work at home do so not for some self-indulgent reason, but to help the family. They want to raise the kids instead of sending them to day care. They want to care for ailing parents or an ill spouse. Or they have a disability that prevents them from holding a traditional job, but still want the feelings of accomplishment and fulfillment that come with working. Yet, they still feel guilty about taking time away from others to put toward their work-at-home goal.

For some women, time is filled with other activities because of poor planning and a lack of prioritizing. Whatever the reason, time is a commodity that can't be wasted. To be successful you need to:

1. Make working at home a priority. You don't have to put your goal above God or family, but it does mean cutting back on some activities and saying no to others.

2. MAKE time instead of finding time. Don't wait for moments of free time because they're fleeting. When they do arrive, they are short lived and not used to their full potential.

3. Protect your work-at-home time. When you schedule time to work on your goal, don't allow other things to get in the way.

LAWS OF WORK-AT-HOME SUCCESS #②
Don't find time, MAKE time to work at home.

So how do you go about making more time? Part of that depends on how much time you need to work. Do you plan on jumping in with both feet, working at home full time? Or will you work part time or moonlight around your regular job? Regardless of your time constraints, here are some tips for making more time:

1. Keep track of the time you're using now. When do you get up? How much time do you spend at each activity? Don't guestimate how you use your time, as most people make gross errors in calculations when they do. They indicate they watch only an hour of television a day when in fact they watch the show before and/or after the one they wanted to watch. So write down how you use your time as you go through your day to get an accurate picture of your time use.

2. Ask yourself what you are willing to give up for the next year or so to be able to work at home.

3. Use your time wisely. It's not the amount of time; it's how you use the time. It is possible to earn an income from home working a few hours a day, but the work must be focused on the activities that make money. Surfing the Internet, reading e-mail, and moving papers from one pile to the next isn't working.

Plan for Work-at-Home Success

1. Make a list or write a narrative about your reasons for wanting to work at home. Make it compelling so that you can feel the burning desire to reach your goal. You may even want to post your reasons in your office to help keep you inspired and motivated.

2. Keep a time log to find areas where you can make time for your work-at-home project.

3. Work on developing the habits and traits needed to succeed.

4. Buy a new pair of pajamas or other comfortable wear to inspire you.

CHAPTER TWO

The Best Way to Work at Home

EVERY DAY I GET E-MAIL THAT ASKS ONE OF TWO questions. The first is, "Do you know where I can work at home typing or doing data entry?" Aside from the fact that the odds of finding a typing or data entry job are practically nil, is the reality that by limiting a job search to just these types of work, people are missing out on dozens of better opportunities.

The second question I get is, "What is the best work-at-home option?" I usually interpret "best" to mean, "what will make the most money in the least amount of time, with minimal effort and investment?" My answer is always, "The best work-at-home option for you is the one that you will do."

There are hundreds of ways that you can make money from home. Some of them could potentially make you rich, but many of them you may not be willing do to. I know people who make obscene amounts of money in network marketing. But for most people, the words "network marketing" send them running for the hills. So while network marketing is the best option for some, it's the worst for others. This is true for all work-at-home options, whether it's telecommuting, selling on eBay, or building a business from scratch. Success at working from home isn't about the opportunity you choose (as long as you choose something legal); it's about whether or not you'll do it.

LAW OF WORK-AT-HOME SUCCESS #③
Working from home isn't about the program you choose; it's about whether or not you'll do it.

The problem with looking for typing or data entry work or searching for the "best" work-at-home opportunity is that it most likely will lead to scams. Further, choosing an opportunity based on money or ease usually fails because the people who join them aren't really invested in the product or service. Wanting to make money or be rich isn't bad, it's the love of money that is bad. But going after the money as the primary goal without considering what's involved and what it takes to succeed doesn't work. The network marketing example is proof of this. Many people want the opportunity that network marketing provides, but don't believe in the product or service they are promoting or don't want to talk to people or sell. Since network marketing is all about word-of-mouth referrals, which requires knowledge and enthusiasm about the product and talking to people, you can see why so many people who join for the money fail.

So what is the best way to go about making money at home? The best way to find work from home is to tap into what you already know, do, or love. That's it. I used my background in social work to find a telecommuting job as an adoption worker.

I used my experiences in working at home and my interest in teaching to create a successful website and now a book. Mrs. Fields loved cookies. J. K. Rowling had a great story rattling around in her head, and ten years later is the richest woman in England. Julie Aigner-Clark wanted to expose her babies to the arts, so she developed Baby Einstein, and in five years had $20 million in sales and sold the company to Disney.

Except for J. K. Rowling, these ladies probably did very little typing or data entry. Further, they didn't start out focused on becoming bazillionaires. Sure they may have wanted to make money, but each took something they had experience in or were passionate about, and turned it into their very own pot of gold. Maybe you don't want to earn a million dollars, or maybe you do. The point is that if you find something that you can get excited about and you're willing to put in the time and effort to achieve its fruition, the money will come. In fact, if you're good at and enjoy it, you'll not only make money faster, you'll likely make more money than choosing something outside your knowledge base or experience.

If you're thinking that you don't have the skills or knowledge to work at home, think again. You don't need a college degree or special certificates to use your experiences. If you have lived your life this far, you've picked up skills and experiences that you can use to find or create a home-based career. And surely you have interests or hobbies you enjoy that can be turned into money makers. All these things are your assets; things that you can use to create income.

Work with What You Know

What do you know? What do you like to do? What are you passionate about? What would really excite you and have you jumping out of bed instead of rolling over and hitting the snooze button? Your first step to work-at-home success will be to inventory your skills and experiences, as well as your talents and interests.

Don't skip these worksheets. You'll be using the information from them throughout the rest of the book.

The Education and Experience Worksheet

Fill in the worksheet below listing all the experiences you can think of. If you need more copies, visit the Work-at-Home Success website at *www.workathomesuccess.com* to download this and other worksheets.

1. Educational background. Where did you attend college and what degrees have you earned? What courses have you taken even if you haven't earned a degree? Don't worry if it's a class in underwater basket weaving or some other topic you don't think offers a marketable skill. There are 115,000 websites about underwater basket weaving and you never know when one of them will need help. Include the names of the schools and the dates of attendance, including the year you earned your degree.

2. Work experience. Write down all experience, even if it's something you don't think can be done at home. You'd be surprised at how many jobs today can be done from home, so don't limit yourself. Write down everything from babysitting to cashier and beyond. Include information on where you worked, your job title, the dates or number of years you held the job, and your duties and responsibilities involved in the job. Be specific when listing the duties of your jobs and include activities that may not be in your job description. These are the actual activities you were paid to do and often they can be performed at other jobs. As a babysitter you managed people, handled crises, and

maintained order. As a cashier you gained experience working with the public and providing customer support.

3. Volunteer or internship experience. Again, don't leave anything out. Did you help in a retirement home, serve meals to the homeless, or rock babies in the neonatal intensive care unit at the hospital? Include where you worked, for how long, and what tasks you were involved in doing.

4. Memberships to associations. Are you the president of your homeowners' association (many owners' associations employ home workers) or treasurer of your local Junior League? Include offices held, dates of membership, and other important information.

5. Professional Certifications. Do you have a real estate license? Are you a certified financial planner? Indicate what certifications were earned, dates they are valid, and other important information.

6. Awards. Include awards or recognition you have received. For example, if you received the Employee of the Year at your job, you want to include that. If you received Player of the Year in your recreational soccer league, go ahead and write it down. Perhaps a soccer association is looking for a knowledgeable soccer player to employ.

7. Other skills and experiences not included elsewhere. Have you built websites using HTML, but never had training or a job in website programming? Can you speak a foreign language (there are many jobs for translators)? We all have job skills and experiences that are sometimes dismissed because they were self-taught or not part of a paying job. In the cyber world many employers are open to self-taught and entry-level employees, so write down any other skills you may have, no matter how insignificant they may seem. Include interests as well. Who would ever think that the skill of typing quickly and accurately and an

interest in talk shows could lead to a job? Yet closed captioning jobs are springing up all over the place.

Next, list your hobbies and passions.

What are your hobbies (e.g., gardening, reading, scrapbooking, car restoration, etc)?

1._____

2._____

3._____

4._____

5._____

What are you passionate about (e.g., wellness, ending poverty, politics, etc.)?

1._____

2._____

3._____

4._____

5._____

Finally, identify skill sets and traits you possess that are needed to successfully work at home. Simply put a check mark next to the skills or traits you have.

Information Processing
Gathering info
Compiling info
Organizing info
Managing info
Analyzing info
Assessing info
Presenting info

Leadership Skills
Managing projects
Managing people .
Initiating projects
Problem-solving skills
Initiative
Negotiating skills
Motivational skills

Communication Skills
Written communication
Oral communication
Presentation skills
Instructing skills
Group-discussion skills
Interviewing skills

Traits
Adaptable
Assertive
Competent
Cooperative
Creative
Decisive
Dependable
Diligent
Diplomatic
Discreet
Energetic
Experienced
Expert
Flexible
Knowledgeable
Outgoing
Perceptive
Professional
Punctual
Reliable
Resourceful
Responsible
Self-motivated
Thorough
Versatile

Creating Your Perfect Career

We'll be using all the above information in more detail later to help you identify specific work options in the Telecommuting and Home Business sections. However, I want to illustrate how many options are available to you using the results from the worksheets. The chart below uses the hobby of gardening to provide ideas on how money can be made through gardening products, services, and information in a job or home business.

Work-at-Home Ideas in Gardening

Gardening	Services	Product	Information
Job	Copywriting for garden business	Sell garden products	Gardening articles
Job	Web design for garden business		
Job	Customer Service for garden business		
Home Business	Landscape business	Create gardening products	Gardening books
Home Business	Teach gardening	Sell gardening products	Write articles
Online Business	Gardening advice	Gardening products	Ad space or affiliate ads on gardening website

It's okay if you don't understand what all these options mean or if you don't like some of them. The point is that you notice that in one hobby, we have identified fifteen different job types. Fifteen! From one hobby! How many experiences, skills, and interests did you list on your worksheets? Even if it's just five, you have the potential to create fifty different work-at-home jobs or businesses.

How to Avoid Work-at-Home Scams

Before we continue on to work-at-home options, we first need to cover work-at-home scams and how to avoid them.

"Make $400 a week stuffing envelopes!"

Raise your hand if you have ever fallen for that one. If we were in the room together, you'd see my hand up in the air. Yep, I've been scammed. More than once. And over 3 million other people fall for work-at-home scams just online each year, according to a Federal Trade Commission Consumer Fraud Survey. But avoiding work-at-home scams is not hard if you arm yourself with two important skills: knowledge and control over your emotions.

Knowledge Is Power

The more you know about scams, the better prepared you'll be to avoid them. Below is a list of work-at-home scams you absolutely need to avoid. When you see them, don't waste one second pondering if maybe this time it's for real. It won't be. Trust me on this.

- Envelope stuffing
- Assembly work
- Typing (Legitimate typing jobs are usually referred to as transcription or are part of a virtual assistant job.)
- E-mail processing
- Rebate processing
- Data entry (almost always a scam or deceptive scheme)

It seems like every day a new scam is born. So if you find a work-at-home offer that isn't listed above, use the rules below to determine if it's on the up and up.

1.   If it's a job (an offer of employment), NEVER, EVER pay money to get hired. You can invest in a good job database or hire someone to help with your resume, but legitimate employers will never charge to hire you. Think of it this way: If your current boss told you to pay him to put you on payroll or for paperclips, you'd think he was nuts. The same is true in a work-at-home job. Any job ad that asks for money should automatically be deleted.

2.   Never use your personal bank account to help a business with financial transactions. Money transferring and processing schemes have left people destitute and without banking privileges. These scams come in different forms, but all ask you to do the same things: 1) Set up a bank account, 2) deposit a big sum of cash that is sent to you by check (it often looks like a cashier's check), and 3) withdraw the money, minus 10 percent (your payment) and send it to a company or individual. What happens is that a few days to a few months later, your bank informs you that the check you cashed is bogus and now you're liable for ALL the money you just sent (by a real cashier's check) to the scammer. A legitimate company will never ask to use your personal account to help it handle payments.

3.   Never join a home business that is focused only on recruiting or that doesn't have a quality product or service to sell. These programs are pyramid schemes. Legitimate home businesses always have good products and services. It may have a recruiting aspect to its program, but the money earned is always made on product sales.

Control Your Emotions

The information I have supplied about common scams and rules to remember are well publicized; and yet millions of women still fall victim to them. These women aren't ignorant or unintelligent. Frequently, they report having had a niggling feeling that they were sending their money off to a scam. So why did they do it? They did it because the ad they read tapped into their desire to work at home so effectively, their emotional response outweighed their reasoning. This is what the scam artists take advantage of. Scammers are master marketers and brilliant copywriters. They understand the psychology of sales, and they use it to exploit women's desires to work at home. Take a look at the fraudulent ad below:

> *Get Paid $400 a week typing simple entries online. Perfect for moms, students, or retired. Set your own hours. No experience necessary.*

A mother who is heartbroken at taking her children to day care or a retired woman worried about making ends meet will see this ad and think her prayers have been answered. You may see the ad and think, "It's too good to be true so it must be a scam." But think about ads you responded to that weren't on the up and up. Or ads you were tempted to respond to. Despite the skepticism, was there temptation? There was for me. But I sent the money because I wanted so badly to stay home with my children and my emotions overrode my common sense. I justified it by telling myself things like, "The ad has a real address and phone number," or "The person who responded to my e-mail was really helpful." Or, "Surely people type at home; I just haven't found the right company . . . maybe this one is it." That's the type of thinking that scammers are hoping for. They write ads that appeal to a mother's desire to raise her children or to a woman's fear of not being able to support herself. They know that buying is done at an emotional level and later (once the money is sent) is justified with facts.

LAW OF WORK-AT-HOME SUCCESS #④
When searching for work-at-home opportunities, keep your emotions in check to avoid falling for work-at-home scams.

Take a look at the scam ad again:

Get Paid $400 a week typing simple entries online. Perfect for moms, students, or retired. Set your own hours. No experience necessary.

And compare it to a legitimate ad:

Part-time administrative assistant needed to support public relations company. Flexible schedule, 10-20 hours per week. Must have excellent communication skills and be proficient in Word, PowerPoint, Excel, and QuickBooks. Duties include scheduling, mailings, writing cover letters, ordering supplies, invoicing, and accounts payable. Send resume and references.

If you look carefully, you'll see the scam job is a sales ad looking for anybody who will respond, while the legitimate job ad is looking for someone with specific skills and experience. The difference is that the scam ad sounds easy, fast, and simple, and speaks directly to the woman who wants to be at home. It perpetuates the idea that working at home doesn't require work. The real job ad sounds like work; work to get the job and work to do the job.

Don't underestimate the power of your emotions to muddle your mind. Before opening your wallet, learn the rules for avoiding scams and keep your emotions in check.

Plan for Work-at-Home Success

1. Do the skills, experiences, and talent inventory.

2. List hobbies and passions.

3. Begin to brainstorm ideas for products, services, or information related to your skills, knowledge, and interests.

4. Reread and remember the rules for avoiding scams.

5. Make a commitment to yourself to not let your emotions get the best of you.

CHAPTER THREE

Can You Afford NOT to Work at Home?

MANAGING MONEY IS A TEDIOUS JOB. If you're like me, you'd rather not do it. There was a time that I didn't even want to know how much I had, or didn't have as the case turned out to be. But if you're going to work at home, you must become a good money manager. As an incentive to do the money-related activities coming up in this chapter, I'll let you in on a secret: Most people who do these worksheets discover they'll save money by working at home. Even better, they learn that they need to earn far less money than they thought in order to stay home.

The Cost of Working

Some women put off their dream of working at home because they don't have the money. But if you have a traditional job, you already spend money to work on things like gas and pantyhose. In fact, you may be spending more to support your traditional job than you would by working at home. When I worked full time as a social worker in a regular job, I earned $28,000 a year, but my expenses related to work amounted to more than $21,000 a year. No joke. After all work-related expenses and taxes, I took home less than $8,000 a year. No wonder we were broke. Here's where it all went:

Job-Related Expenses

Expenses	Amount
Taxes (federal and state)	$3,000
Child care ($120/week)	$6,000
Commuting (10 miles each way)	$1,700
Appearance (dry cleaning, clothes, work supplies, etc.)	$1,000
Lunch	$1,000
Convenience items (take-out meals, etc.)	$2,600
Pick-me-ups (I deserve this because I work hard.)	$2,400
Newer car plus tax, insurance (extra over the cost of a used car)	$2,400
Total amount spent to work	$21,100

Subtracting the work-related expenses from my salary ($28,000 - $23,100 = $7,900), I discovered that I contributed only $7,900 per year to the family income. That's only $659 per month and $3.80 per hour! I paid more to go to work than I actually brought home! Calculating the cost of your job is particularly important if you are a two-income family with kids or other care expenses, and your spouse is reluctant for you to work at home. When I showed my husband how much we paid for me to work, he was on board with me finding a work-at-home option, as long as we didn't go broke.

What Do You Pay to Work?

Now it's your turn to calculate how much you currently pay to work outside the home. To complete the Cost of Work Worksheet below, you'll need recent paystubs, bank statements, old check registers, and receipts related to child care, gas, car expenses, dining out, and convenience items.

Cost of Work Worksheet
Your Gross Monthly Salary: _____

Expenses Related to Work

Expenses	Amount
Federal taxes	$
State taxes	$
Local taxes	$
Social Security	$
Professional fees/licenses	$
Child care	$
Commuting (toll, parking, 2nd car)	$
Gasoline and mileage	$
Car insurance (extra car, nicer car)	$
Gifts for special friends, etc. at work	$
Convenience food for meals	$
Eating out	$
Housekeeping help	$
Grooming needs (hair, nails, etc.)	$
Guilt items for kids and family	$
Extra cost related to lack of time to research cheaper prices	$
Extra cost related to hiring help instead of making repairs yourself	$
Total expenses related to work	$

Actual contribution to family income (salary minus total work expenses) _____

What did you discover? Do you spend more to work outside of the home than you actually keep? Does one-half or three-quarters of your income go to work-related expenses? Hopefully at this point you're horrified at how little you actually take home, and thrilled that you won't have to earn as much to work at home. But don't quit your day job yet.

How Much Money Do You Need to Live?

I hate budgeting because I'm not very good at it. But without budgeting, I'd probably be in the red and looking for a job. Having an understanding of my family's spending is critical to my being able to work at home, and it will be for you, too.

In today's world it is not uncommon for people to be living beyond their means. If you find you are running out of money before you run out of month or you are paying bills hoping the check won't be cashed before you get paid, then you're probably living beyond your means. If this is the case, it's critical that you determine your financial fitness and learn exactly what it would take for you to afford to work at home.

Even if you are not having financial problems, it is wise to have a detailed understanding of your finances as you start your new venture.

To complete the budget worksheet that follows, you'll need bank statements, copies of receipts, bills, and other documents that outline what you spend on average each month. Input your current expenses under the column "Current Spending." You can ignore the "Goal Spending" for now.

Household Budget

Expenses	Current Spending	Goal Spending
Mortgage/Rent	$	$
Homeowner association fees	$	$
Property tax (usually included in mortgage)	$	$
Home insurance	$	$
Electric utility	$	$
Gas utility	$	$
Water	$	$
Sewer	$	$
Telephone	$	$
Cell phone	$	$
Internet	$	$
Home maintenance	$	$
Other home-related expenses	$	$
Life insurance	$	$
Medical insurance	$	$
Medical copayments	$	$
Dental insurance	$	$
Vision insurance	$	$
Other medical-related expenses	$	$
Car payments	$	$
Car insurance	$	$
Personal property tax	$	$
Car registration fees	$	$
Car maintenance	$	$
Gasoline	$	$
Consumer credit payments	$	$
Student loan payments	$	$
Other debts	$	$
Child support	$	$
Alimony	$	$
Clothes	$	$
Grocery	$	$

Dining out	$	$
Lunch	$	$
Cable TV service	$	$
Video rentals or purchases	$	$
Excursions (weekend fun)	$	$
Magazine subscriptions	$	$
Vacation	$	$
Hobbies	$	$
Grooming (haircuts, etc.)	$	$
Dry cleaning	$	$
Gifts	$	$
Cash withdrawals	$	$
Emergency	$	$
Savings and retirement funding	$	$
Other expenses	$	$

Total up your expenses to discover your current monthly spending. Remember that some of these expenses such as gas and dry cleaning can be reduced or eliminated by working at home. At this point, you just want to know how much money is leaving the household bank right now.

How Much Do You Need to Make?

So far you've calculated how much money you spend to work and live. Next, you need to find out how much you need to earn to stay home. This is where things got really exciting for me. When I did this exercise, I found that to work at home, I needed to earn half the amount I'd originally thought. It was a turning point for me because up until then, I didn't really believe I'd be able to do it. Thinking I had to earn over $2,000 a month to stay home, and then discovering I needed to earn only $900 changed everything. Nine hundred dollars was doable.

So let's see what you need to earn to stay home. If you're single without another source of income, the total of your expenses is what you need to earn. If you're married, have a partner, or another source of income, take the number representing your total monthly expenses and subtract the second source of income. For example, if your total household expense is currently $3,000 and your spouse makes $2,000 per month, the remaining amount is $1,000 ($3,000 expenses – $2,000 spouse income = $1,000). This amount is what you need to earn to stay home. Or is it?

Remember, you'll save or eliminate some expenses by not working. Reduce or subtract the specific work-related expenses on your Household Expense Budget, putting the new number in the "Goal Spending" column. For example, if you spend $400 a month on gas but would drive a third as much if you stayed home, your goal spending for gas would be $267 per month ($133 in savings). Estimate new figures on all your work-related expenses from the Cost of Work Worksheet you did earlier, putting them in the "Goal Spending" column of the budget.

You now have a new number for your monthly expenses. Use it to subtract the second income, if you have one. Now how much do you need to earn?

What if you could earn less and still stay home?

When I did these exercises, it occurred to me that the more I saved, the less I needed to earn at home. So I returned to my budget and found ways to reduce my expenses even more. For example, I spent $434 ($100 per week) on groceries (this was in the late 1990s). With some savvy consumer shopping tips, I was able to cut my food bill by another 20 percent, saving me $92.80 per month.

Researching and reading about savings ideas, I was able to cut expenses on food, utilities, entertainment, and more. The result was that to stay home, I only had to make $575 a month instead of the $2,000 I'd originally thought I'd need to earn. I could continue to work forty hours a week to take home less than half my salary or I could work from home part time, be with my kids, and earn about the same. Guess what I chose to do?

Some women who do this exercise are able to cut their expenses down so much that they don't have to work at all. Others don't want to make so many cuts in the family budget. It's all a matter of what you are willing to do. I was willing to sell my new car and replace it with a less expensive used one. I still had to work, but I needed to earn $200 less a month and I was able to quit my job that much sooner.

Return to your budget and identify areas where you can cut your expenses. Start by reducing expenses in categories that aren't set, such as groceries and utilities. After that, find ways to reduce spending in other areas. Can you refinance your home for a cheaper mortgage rate? Can you reduce your taxes? Do you really need a second car or a second car with a payment?

When looking for areas where you can save, remember that you don't have to live like a hermit. Look at it as a challenge to locate the cheapest ways to do everything from buying clothes to going on family outings. Take your new "Goal Spending" number and subtract the amount of other income your family receives. This is the new amount you need to earn. For example, if your household now needs $2,400 a month to cover expenses and your spouse earns $2,000 a month, you need to make (or find a way to save) $400 per month.

The Final Number

You're almost done! Hopefully, as awful as budgeting is, the numbers you're calculating are inspiring you to keep going. You have just one more money-related calculation.

The budget has helped you determine what you need to earn from home by eliminating your work-related and extraneous expenses. However, if you're going to work at home, you will have some expenses related to your job or business. At this point, you don't know what those expenses will be, so as you progress through the book and evaluate different work-at-home options, develop a list of expenses related to those options. Even in a telecommuting job you'll have a few expenses, whether it's Internet access, buying software, or taxes. Use the questions below to help you calculate the expenses of work-at-home options you consider:

- What type of work will you be doing?
- What is the normal salary or income for that type of work?
- Will you pay or will your employer deduct taxes on your income?
- What (estimated) will your tax and social security contributions be?
- Will an employer be providing health insurance or other benefits? Will there be any cost to you?
- Will you need to purchase any equipment to work at home?
- Are there any professional dues or fees associated with the job or business?
- Will you need part time child care?
- What other expenses will there be?

Once you have evaluated a work-at-home option including potential expenses, add the work-related expenses to the amount you need to earn to stay home to find the total amount of money you need to earn from home. Even with work-at-home expenses added back in, your needed income should still be less than what you'd need to earn working outside the home.

Plan for Work-at-Home Success

Now is the time for you to discover how much (or little) you make and whether or not you can improve your financial situation by working at home!

1. Gather all the materials and supplies you need for completing the budgets such as bank statements, check registers, bills, pay stubs, etc.

2. Do the Cost of Work Worksheet.

3. Create a budget showing how much you need to live on.

4. Determine how much you need to make to afford to work at home.

5. Find ways to reduce your budget and recalculate how much you'd need to stay home.

6. Keep track of expenses you'll incur as you develop your work at home idea and add that back into your budget.

7. Stand up. Stretch. And do a dance. The money exercises are done for now!

CHAPTER FOUR

Making Working at Home Work for You and Your Family

WORKING AT HOME WILL MAKE MANY THINGS IN LIFE EASIER, while other things will become more difficult. You'll be faced with new distractions, challenges, and obstacles. The best way to meet these new challenges is to anticipate and plan for them.

Getting Spousal Support

I'm very fortunate to have a husband who has been supportive of my work-at-home dream, even when it caused financial stress. But I have spoken to many women whose husbands need a little more convincing than mine did. In fact, one of the biggest hurdles women face when wanting to work at home comes from family members. It's hard enough to create a home-based career, but an unsupportive spouse can make it nearly impossible. Here are some tips to convince your husband to support your work-at-home goal:

■ *Involve him.* Let your spouse help with finding the right opportunity, setting goals, and even reaping the rewards.

■ *Share the details.* Have your spouse read all the materials you read, listen to any recordings or calls you attend, and talk to people you talk to so he can get the same information you do. Any questions or concerns can be raised and explored together.

■ *Share your plan.* Some husbands worry that the family will end up in the poorhouse if you quit your job to work at home. Make a plan to show that you won't let the family finances suffer. Your plan should include where you'll find the time and money to begin a work-at-home job or business, as well as the potential benefits.

■ *Plan for household management.* Working at home takes time; time that your spouse may expect you to spend with family or on housework. Make a plan to show your husband how the rest of life can be managed and indicate areas that you could use support.

■ *Make a schedule of work and nonwork hours and stick to it.* Don't let your work-at-home venture take too much time away from your family, but ask your family to respect your work hours.

■ *Let your spouse know working at home is important to you . . . if it is.* Sometimes work-at-home ventures, especially those run by women, are perceived as hobbies. It's okay if it is a hobby, but if you're looking to make it your career or if it's important to you, convey that to your husband. Hopefully he'll respect your dream even if he doesn't agree with it.

■ *Tell your spouse how it will be different this time around.* If you have a history of failed attempts at working at home, getting spousal support can be difficult. Along with doing the six other items listed above, be sure you're making good choices AND doing the work! Evaluate why your past efforts failed and be completely honest about your part in the failure. Then make a plan that shows how it will be different this time around.

■ *Consider doing it anyway.* If your spouse is holding you back, take a good look at why. It may be that one of the suggestions above will help him understand what it is you're trying to accomplish. But if not, sometimes you just need to do it anyway.

If you go the "I'm doing it no matter what" route, you still want to do the seven steps outlined above because it will not only help ensure your success, but it will let your spouse know that you are aware of his concerns and are trying to alleviate them.

Working at Home with Children

Working at home with children can be difficult. This is another area that many women fail to truly evaluate. It's very, very difficult to work with constant interruption followed by guilt when you tell the kids to leave you alone. Therefore, you'll need to consider some sort of child care arrangement.

The amount and type of child care you'll need will depend on the age of your children and the amount of time you need to work. Infants and preschoolers in particular will need more supervised care. It is not feasible to fit in a forty-hour workweek working during your children's nap times. On the other hand, you can, as a work-at-home parent, take advantage of sleep times and thus require less child care than in an office job.

School-age children require less care because they are in school during the day. But if you find the school day is not long enough for you to get your work done, consider hiring a babysitter to come by after school or involve your children in after-school activities that can give you more time to work. During the summer, consider day camps and other activities to keep your kids entertained. It costs money, but it prevents them from spending the whole summer on the computer or in front of the TV.

There are many child care options available to work-at-home parents. These include:

■ *Morning preschool programs.* Some programs take children as young as eighteen months old.

■ *Play groups or babysitting co-ops operated by member parents.* Each parent takes a turn providing care, but the benefits of having parents you know and trust to watch your children is invaluable.

■ *Hire a teenager or retired person to come in for a few hours a day.* This allows your children to stay in their own environment, but you can work without providing supervision.

■ *Use community programs and activities* such as day camps, after-school child care, and recreational sports to gain a few hours or even a day to work.

■ *Work during your children's sleep hours* before they wake, after they're in bed, or during nap time.

If you have to parent and work at the same time, develop strategies to keep the kids busy while you work. It sounds easy, but in fact, this has been the most difficult part of working at home for me. My children settle down to play or watch a video, but ten minutes later they want a drink or need help with something or are stuck. Even though they know I'm working, these little "emergencies" cause them to interrupt me. The result is that I get frustrated and then I feel guilty for not being available to them. Here are some ideas to help you work while children are at home:

- *Set a timer* and let them know you will spend time with them when the timer goes off.
- *Have special work-time activities that they will enjoy, but require little supervision.* These activities may include stickers, coloring, games, videos, or special toys.
- *Allow children to lick stamps, open mail,* or do other work to help you.
- *Set up a mini-office for your child* with paper, phone, pencils, etc. so they can play office.

LAW OF WORK-AT-HOME SUCCESS #⑤
Enlist the family's help and support for your work-at-home goal!

Establishing a Work Routine

When people think about working at home, work is often the last thing that comes to mind. Instead, they focus on sleeping late, not having to put on makeup, taking the kids to the park, and the other perks related to working at home. But working at home is only successful if you work. To maximize your work performance as well as to take advantage of the perks of working at home, establishing a work routine is a must. Some things to consider include:

What are your peak working hours? Are you most coherent in the morning and sluggish in the afternoon? Set up your work schedule so that the most intensive work is completed in the morning. What motivates you? During those times when it's hard to get to work, what can get you focused? Music? Coffee? Stretching? Thinking of the commute you'll have if you don't work? You need to set realistic goals. Don't try to do an entire week's worth of work in one morning. Pace yourself, keeping in mind your peak working hours.

Organize Your Home and Office

The main advantage to commuting to a job is that it creates a natural barrier between work and home. Living and working in one place doesn't have this. It's not unusual for me to put a load of laundry in, check my e-mail, wash the dishes, and upload a new web page all in that order. However, sometimes intermingling home and work life results in none of the above getting done. The best way to make working and living in one place work is to get organized. Here are some helpful tricks:

- *Create a master schedule for all family events.* Use a calendar with enough room to write all meetings, appointments, activities, and events for the whole family. Include your work and off hours as well. I like the calendars that have a grid (mom-oriented calendars have this) in which each member of the family can have a place for their events. Or you can use a planner or computer-based organizers. Choose a system that works for you, but that your family has access to as well. Your schedule should be fixed, but flexible when someone is sick or other obligations present themselves.

- *Set up a regular schedule for family chores such as laundry, bills, grocery shopping, etc.* It may seem very domestic to have a grocery and laundry day, but you'll be glad when you never run out of food or underwear.

- *Establish a yearly schedule for big chores* such as car maintenance, service on the heating and air systems, spring cleaning, etc.

- *Schedule time for running errands to the post office or bank.* That way you don't feel like you are losing work time to get it done.
- *Enlist the family's help in household duties.* Even young children can pick up toys, sort socks, and set the table. Make children responsible for themselves in the morning. To help, set up a specific routine. Kids should have one place for backpacks so there is no mad search for them in the morning. Completed homework should be put in the backpack as soon as it's finished.
- *Consider cooking several meals at one time and freezing the extras.* This can save you time and money in the long run.
- *Get rid of household clutter.* It just gets in your way and slows you down.

Staying Focused

Freedom is an awesome responsibility. Some find the freedom of working at home without the boundaries of schedules, office cubicles, and a set routine too difficult and end up going back to work. I don't get it. But I do agree that working at home requires a great deal of discipline and organization. You would be surprised how a one-hour lunch break to watch a favorite TV show turns into three hours. Or how distracting dishes and laundry can be. To keep focused on your work:

- *Create and stick to a schedule.* Post it where everyone can see and honor it . . . even you.
- *Set goals and rewards.*
- *Use doors to hide laundry and other distractions.*
- *Use voice mail to screen calls.*
- *Post inspirational quotes or pictures of your goals over your desk to remind you of what you're working toward.*

One Is a Lonely Number

Being the boss of your own time can be a wonderful thing. But it can be lonely as well. The work-at-home office is devoid of office politics, water cooler gossip, and other social opportunities. Further, there is little feedback, kudos, or support. To keep from feeling lonely in your solitude, it's helpful to develop connections with others. Just because you work for yourself doesn't mean you have to work by yourself. Stay connected to the office or your network. This will keep you in good favor with the boss and clients. It can also keep you in the "gossip" loop and notified of social functions such as the office Christmas party.

Join a business organization. Groups such as the chamber of commerce not only provide opportunities for marketing and training, but social outlets as well.

Build a support network. Find other women in your area who work from home to organize a coffee day. Websites like Meetup.com offer ways to find people in your neighborhood with whom you can meet for fun or support. You can also build support networks online through any of the social networking sites like MySpace.com, Facebook.com, or other business mastermind groups. It is important to get out of the house. Try to reserve one day a week just for you. If you want to work on this day, do it somewhere else. Go to the bookstore or café, read, drink coffee, and do a little work.

Plan for Emergencies

There will come a day when your quiet workday will be interrupted by a sick child or a rush project. The car will break down or your computer will crash. The best way to deal with these times is to anticipate and plan for them. If you need to go into the office or take on extra work, make arrangements for your child. Do you have a friend you can call at the last minute?

Can your spouse take a day off? Is there an after-school program your child can go to?

If your boss or clients need to see your work right away, you don't want to waste time wading through piles of papers or searching your computer hard drive. Have a briefcase or tote boxes that you can transport your work materials in on short notice. Back up all copies of your work to a CD or flash drive to use at the office or take advantage of websites offering free storage space. Keep your work and home equipment and appliances in tip-top shape. Have a toolbox or a list of technicians on hand to help when things break down.

If you are in a last-minute bind to complete work and need to sacrifice some family time, enlist your family's help. Let them know ahead of time that there may be situations in which you need to work instead of cook dinner or go to the park. Ready them for these times by having frozen meals and activities to occupy the children already prepared.

Forge Ahead

Murphy's Law states that whatever can go wrong will go wrong. While you'll have successes, I can guarantee that you'll experience setbacks, failures, and disappointments as well. You won't get the job you want. Your foolproof ad campaign will fizzle. It's a fact of life that stuff happens. However, the successful home-based worker doesn't use these setbacks as reasons to quit. Instead, she sees them as challenges to overcome. That can be easier said than done. Here are some tips to keep looking up when the world is bringing you down:

■ *Realize what didn't work.* Analyze what's going on to find what's not working. Does your resume or ad need to be improved? Do you need to find more time?

- *Record all the actions you've taken to reach your goal.* You may be surprised to discover that you haven't done as much as you think you have.
- *Keep your eye on the prize.*
- *Make a deal with yourself.* Commit to more time or a new effort, and reward yourself when you see results.

LAW OF WORK-AT-HOME SUCCESS #6
Stuff happens. Know it. Prepare for it. Work through it!

Keep Learning

Ten years ago, Internet marketing resources suggested using pop-ups and bulk e-mail to build your traffic and business. Today they are considered no-no's and instead there is a list of newer, more effective marketing options. Failure to keep on top of current trends will not only lead to missing out on new ways to make money, but in the Internet example above, can cost you business. For that reason, dedicating a part of your work effort to learning is vital to your success.

Keeping abreast of current trends related to your work will ensure that you're a needed and valuable resource, as well as position you as an expert, thereby increasing your value and credibility. Ways to keep learning include reading books, magazines, blogs, news items (online and off), listening to radio shows and podcasts, and attending seminars and workshops. Topics you study should cover your industry as well as business, success and self-help, money management, and personal productivity.

Plan for Work-at-Home Success

1. Have a discussion with your spouse about working at home. Address his concerns and enlist his help.

2. Make child care plans or find ways to keep the kids busy while you work.

3. Create schedules, routines, and systems to help manage the home and home office.

4. Develop ways to stay connected to the world to fend off loneliness.

5. Anticipate and plan for emergencies and problems.

6. Set aside time every day to expand your knowledge.

CHAPTER FIVE

Home Sweet Home Office

HAVING A HOME OFFICE IS MORE THAN JUST HAVING A SPACE AND A COMPUTER. If you intend to make your work-at-home career your main source of income, you need a home office designed for efficiency, comfort, and safety.

Finding Space

My first official home office was in the coat closet of my living room. It was actually a pretty good space. The computer cart fit with all the peripherals and I had a shelf for books. Nevertheless, I don't recommend it as a long-term office solution. It didn't work because the closet was in the living room where the TV and toys were housed, creating distractions when I worked. And when I wasn't working, I could still see it, so I was constantly reminded of work I should be doing.

The ideal home office is in a room separate from the rest of the living areas, preferably with a door. You want to be able to set a firm boundary between your living and working spaces. A door lets you close shop when you're off duty or keep the rest of the world out while you're working. The room should have good light, including natural light, and it should offer enough space for you to house everything you need to do your work, including your materials or inventory if you'll have any. Finally, if you'll be seeing clients in your home, create a space separate from the rest of the home that's inviting and comfortable.

Home Furnishings

When putting together a home office, focus first on the furniture needed to get the job done. For most offices that starts with a desk. Desks are like purses—it takes time to find just the right one. You want enough space to do your work and house materials needed for quick access, but not too much space that it becomes another junk room.

Next you need a chair. But not just any chair. You need a quality chair that is comfortable and offers good back support. Often because working at home is seen as a hobby and therefore not worth the expense, people buy low-quality chairs. This is a mistake. If working at home is going to be your career, even if it's just ten hours a week, you need a good-quality chair for safety and comfort.

Storage and or shelving can help you organize all your equipment and materials. I use a large bookshelf for my books as well as housing my printer. I have shelves over my desk for books that I like to reference frequently such as a dictionary or materials related to what I'm currently working on.

The final piece of necessary furniture is a file cabinet to save and organize your tax receipts, client files, articles from magazines, and other resources you need to access. Choose one that is sturdy and balanced. I've had poor-quality file cabinets that fell over if more than one drawer was open. If you'll be handling private information on clients, get a file cabinet that locks.

Computer

Many people start working at home using their existing computer system. However, if your computer is old, or you don't have a computer, save your pennies to get a new one.

I could tell you exactly the specifications you need in buying a computer; however, that information will be out of date tomorrow. Well, maybe not tomorrow, but by the time this book is released there will be faster, stronger, and less-expensive computers available. Instead, consider these items while choosing a good computer:

1. What do you need your computer to do? Make a list of what you'll need your computer to do in relation to your work, such as word processing, accounting, e-mailing, desktop publishing, web design, etc.

2. Make note of the computer requirements of the software you're using as well as any software you intend to buy. Audio and video programs in particular need lots of RAM and storage to run efficiently. Get as much processor speed, RAM, and hard-drive storage as you can afford, as this regulates how fast your computer runs and how easily it can multitask without making you wait.

3. Use the list of features you need on your computer to help you choose other specifications such as CD/DVD players, wireless technology, graphic or video cards, and USB ports (used to plug in your printer and other peripheral equipment).

4. Laptop versus desktop. Desktops usually deliver the most features for the most affordable price, but laptops give you the ability to work in your favorite café or out on the deck. Plus it makes a great portable DVD player when you travel. Because

laptops are so affordable and offer a lot of great features, I recommend going that route if you can.

5. Monitors can be used with desktops as well as laptops. Some companies package the computer and monitor together, however it is possible to buy them separately. Your monitor should be big enough and set to a comfortable height on your desk to avoid eye and neck strain. The LCD flat-panel monitors are more expensive but look cooler and take up less room.

6. Keyboards often come with the complete desktop computer system. If not, or if you'd like to connect a keyboard to your laptop when you're working at your desk, test out a variety of keyboards, as they vary significantly. Some require more pressure than others to press the keys. Some are ergonomically designed while others have keys scrunched up together. Consider getting a wireless keyboard to eliminate cable clutter.

7. A mouse is another item that often comes with a desktop computer. On a laptop, it's located on the keyboard. I have a tiny travel mouse for when I use my laptop on the road because I don't like using the mouse pad on my computer. Like the keyboard, if you're going to buy a mouse, test a few to see if they have the features you want and are comfortable to use. Wireless ones are available as well.

Printers

Today, many printers are also included with the purchase of a computer. If you won't be doing much printing and don't need high-quality print, these low cost ink-jet printers will work fine. However, if your print output will be high or you need high-quality print, spend a little more for a faster, higher resolution printer. Laser printers are now affordable and worth considering. Before making your purchase, check out the cost of replacement ink cartridges and toner, and include these expenses in with your decision about which brand and model of printer to buy.

Fax Machine

It's possible to run your business without a fax machine. Many computers come with a program that can allow you to fax your documents or you can use a free (or paid) service through eFax.com, which will give you a fax number and deliver a fax to you by e-mail. If you don't send or receive faxes on a regular basis, this will be enough.

Copier

If you make frequent trips to the office or copy store to use the copier, consider getting a copier. While most small home-office size copiers are not designed for large jobs, if you have many small jobs, having a copier can save time, money, and travel. Weigh all your copying needs such as frequency of copying, number of copies, and any special features such as double-sided copies to determine the best choice for you. You may decide that a copier isn't cost effective. If that is the case, copy centers often provide pickup and delivery copy services for business purposes.

Scanner

Scanners are great for copying items that need to be faxed via computer, e-mailed, or loaded onto an Internet site. If you have the space, a flatbed scanner will offer you the best versatility over a scanner that requires you to feed the paper through it.

All-in-One Machines

These machines offer all the features of copying, printing, scanning, and faxing without having to buy a separate machine for each. They can be purchased with laser or ink-jet printing. And, they are affordable. The only drawback is that if one feature such as the copier breaks, all the other features may not function either.

Software

Your software needs will depend on the work you do. Common needs include a word processing and e-mail program. Other needs may include contact management, database, spreadsheet, and desktop publishing programs. Determining your software needs requires that you answer the following questions:

- What work will you be doing?
- What software is required to do the work?
- What software is required by the employer or business?

One program you absolutely can't live without is virus protection. It's hard to believe that there are people who spend their time creating programs to purposefully corrupt your machine. (Why can't they use their talents for good instead of evil?) The only way to protect your computer and your work is to have a good virus-protection program and keep it up to date. When choosing a program, pick one that has automatic virus definition updates so you don't have to remember to download them. Virus definitions are what the program uses to identify viruses when scanning your machine or e-mail. Since new viruses are spreading all the time, make sure your machine is able to scan for the latest outbreak.

Also, choose virus-protection software that allows you to schedule scans of your machine so you don't have to remember to do it. Lastly, check that the program will scan your e-mail as it is downloaded or opened, and as it goes out. This is particularly important if you use Outlook, Outlook Express, or other e-mail programs that download your e-mail to your computer.

You will want to invest in a word-processing program, like Microsoft Word. Or get the Open Office Suite for free at *www .openoffice.org*.

Another good investment would be a money-management software program. Working at home can involve irregular pay-days. A money-management program will track your finances to avoid a shortage. Further, if you have a business, a money-management program can track invoices, income sources, and other tasks related to running a home business.

LAW OF WORK-AT-HOME SUCCESS #⑦
Protect your computer with robust virus-protection software that automatically updates and scans your computer!

Internet Access

It's hard to believe that some people still have dial-up service to access the Internet, but many of the other options aren't available or reliable in all areas. Use dial-up Internet access only as your last resort. Many telecommuting jobs require a high-speed service, and to work efficiently on the Internet you really need to work without having to wait for your browser to load.

DSL service is a high-speed Internet option that uses your phone line. You'll need a DSL modem supplied by the service provider. If your computer has a wireless modem, you can buy a wireless router to access your DSL service and avoid tripping over phone cords. It also allows you to access the Internet anywhere in your home (bedroom, porch, etc.) or in cafés with wireless service. Unfortunately, DSL service isn't available in all areas. Call your local phone company or do a search on the Internet to see if you have DSL service where you live.

Another option is cable Internet service that uses the same lines that your cable television service uses. Theoretically, cable Internet service offers faster download speeds, as cable lines have greater bandwidths than DSL. However, cable lines are shared, so speeds may fluctuate depending on how many other users are on the line. Like DSL, cable Internet service can be set up to work through a network and wirelessly. Contact your cable company to inquire about cable Internet service.

A final, out-of-this-world option is satellite Internet service. It's slower than cable or DSL as a result of the lag time involved in traveling to space and back. Further, it tends to be more expensive and depending on your area, reception may not be reliable. However, if you're not able to get DSL or cable Internet access, or are in areas in which traditional communication goes down often, then satellite Internet service may be a good choice.

Phones

The only equipment that may be more important than a computer is a phone. Some women make millions in their businesses with the phone as their only tool. Even if you only use your phone occasionally, get one that has good-quality sound and a variety of features such as mute, flash, and speaker-phone buttons. Check too that it has a plug for a headset, the ultimate in allowing you to multitask while on the phone.

Aside from your personal line, you may want to consider getting an additional phone line for your work-only calls and fax machine. Your local phone company can install a second line through an existing jack or install a whole new line. The basic cost of the second line is generally the same as your first line. Income-tax regulations prevent you from deducting expenses from your first line (except business-related long-distance calls), but you can take a deduction for the expense of additional lines installed for work purposes. Here are some other issues to consider regarding phone lines and communication:

- *Distinctive ring:* If you don't want to install a second line, you can add the distinctive ring feature on your phone line. For a few dollars each month you can have two phone numbers, each with their own unique ring on one phone line. I use distinctive ring for my fax line. A single ring is a regular phone call, while a double ring lets me know that I'm getting a fax. You can add this feature to your home line to separate personal calls (one ring) from work calls (double ring).
- *DSL:* Digital Subscriber Line (DSL) uses a standard phone line to access the Internet. With DSL you have a direct link to the Internet; when you turn your PC on, you are connected to the Internet. DSL also allows you to be on the phone and Internet at the same time.
- *Voice mail:* If you're frequently out of the office, attending to your children, or on the phone, consider getting voice mail. I use the voice-mail service provided by my phone company, as it tells me when I have a call coming in and when I have a message if I'm on the phone with someone else. Plus I can access my messages from anywhere.
- *Cell phones:* If you want to be available to your boss or clients while you are out of the office, a cell phone is a good option. Cellular phone plans vary considerably, so shop around for a plan that offers the best services and good reception in your area.
- *Headset:* A headset allows you to be on the phone and work at the same time. Newer phones have a plug-in for a headset, so all you need is the headset itself, which can be bought for about $10.

■ *Three-way calling:* Three-way calling allows you to be on the phone with two other callers at the same time. If you'll be using three-way calling, add the feature to your phone services, as it's cheaper than paying per use.

Supplying the Home Office

Some women love shoes. Me? I love office supplies. From folders to pens, business cards to paperclips, and doodads to gadgets, the office store has it all for a home office. However, you don't necessarily need it all. If you're an office-supply junkie, be careful about not overdoing it. Before buying your first manila folder and file cabinet, make a list of items you need to do your work. Basic office supplies include:

■ 3-ring binders
■ 3-hole punch
■ Business cards (Vistaprint.com has a variety of affordable—even free—business cards. Or you can make your own.)
■ Calculator (to add up all your moolah!)
■ Correction tape or fluid
■ Envelopes (standard size, various sizes if you'll be shipping materials)
■ Folders
■ Hanging folders and hardware to hang them in the file cabinet
■ Paper (copier, fax, note pads)
■ Paperclips (all sizes)
■ Paper shredder
■ Pens (writing, highlighters, dry erase, permanent markers)
■ Planner (not needed if you use your computer or PDA to organize and plan your day)
■ Printer ink or toner

- Postal scale (if shipping will be a part of your business)
- Recycle bin
- Shipping materials (boxes, packing tape, filler—if shipping will be a part of your business)
- Stamps
- Staples and stapler
- Stationery (you can use a desktop-publishing program to create your own or order it)
- Surge protector (another necessity to prevent damage to your computer!)
- Tape and tape dispenser
- Wastepaper basket

Plan for Work-at-Home Success

1. Make a list of all the equipment, furniture, and supplies you need.

2. Find a space in your home that is free from distraction to set up your home office.

3. Set up your office for comfort and efficiency.

4. Contact the phone or Internet company if you need to install phone lines or Internet access.

Part Two

TELECOMMUTING

CHAPTER SIX

Turn Your Job into a Telecommuting Position

IN 1973, A UNIVERSITY OF SOUTHERN CALIFORNIA PRO-
FESSOR NAMED JACK NILLES came up with the term "telecommuting" to describe a situation in which employees would
work off-site. At the time, the idea of people working at home
was viewed as impractical and unrealistic. You have to remember, in 1973 there were no fax machines or cell phones, and
computers were the size of Mack trucks. Today, nearly a quarter of Americans telecommute and 62 percent who can't telecommute wish they could, according to a Citrix Online survey. Fortunately, telecommuting continues to grow and is found
in companies of all sizes, private and public institutions, and
even in federal, state, and local governments. Experts expect the
trend to continue as telecommuting proves beneficial and even
essential. The growth of telecommuting is fueled by:

■ *Companies working in the global arena* creating a need for skilled and knowledgeable workers all over the world.

■ *Downsizing, which has forced fewer workers to take on more work.* Companies have compensated employees by offering telecommuting as a perk.

■ *Companies needing the best workers,* regardless of where they are located, to stay competitive.

■ *Companies needing to save on real estate* and overhead expenses.

■ *The Americans with Disabilities Act,* which encourages companies to provide opportunities for disabled Americans.

■ *The skills of Generation Xers* who have grown up with computer technology in the home.

■ *The Clean Air Act of 1990 and concerns of global warming.* If only 10 percent of the population telecommuted to work just one day per week, they would conserve about 1.2 million gallons of fuel, and more importantly, prevent nearly 24 million pounds of pollutants from entering the atmosphere . . . per week.

■ *Rise of gas prices.* The United States could save 6 billion gallons of oil each year if all commuters worked from home just one day a week.

■ *Disaster preparedness.* Events such as 9/11, Hurricane Katrina, blizzards, political conventions, and pandemic scares have heightened the need to create systems to maintain communication and infrastructures in the event people can't get to work.

Advantages of Telecommuting

Over thirty years of research on telecommuting shows the advantages of telecommuting to companies are overwhelmingly positive.

- *Money Savings:* Companies can save as much as $10,000 per telecommuter per year.
- *Increased productivity:* Over 70 percent of managers report that telecommuting increases worker productivity by 15 to 20 percent.
- *Improved accountability:* Telecommuting forces managers to evaluate employees on work results and outcomes, not on how long they sit in their cubicle.
- *Reduced absenteeism:* An employee can work at home even if he is feeling under the weather or is home with a sick child. Further, telecommuters take fewer "mental health" days.
- *Retention of valuable employees:* Companies offer telecommuting as a perk to reward and retain valuable employees. These companies understand that it is cheaper to keep a productive employee than to hire and train a new one.
- *Increased competitiveness:* Offering telecommuting programs allows companies to successfully recruit the best employees. Further, telecommuting allows these companies to hire the most qualified employees regardless of the employees' physical location.
- *Earn utility credits:* Government pilot programs have provided incentives to businesses that adopt a telecommuting program as a way to cut down on pollution and congestion.
- *Less downtime during natural disasters,* severe weather, and other events.

The most recent Telework America Survey funded by AT&T found that telecommuters who worked from home (versus a satellite office or on the road) reported the highest levels of productivity, job satisfaction, and commitment to their employers. Telecommuting gives employees:

■ *Flexibility to set their own schedules* and work during their peak performance hours.

■ *More time to pursue other interests* since there is no long commute.

■ *Flexibility and time* to better meet the demands of family life.

■ *Savings on gas, tolls, clothes, lunches out,* and other work-related expenses.

■ *Relief from commuting.*

■ *Relief from office distractions.*

■ *Improved time-management skills.*

■ *Less stress.*

Disadvantages of Telecommuting

While telecommuting offers many advantages to companies and employees, there are some disadvantages as well. These can be overcome, but often present an obstacle to employees trying to create a work-at-home position. Disadvantages of telecommuting to companies include:

■ *Changes in management style:* In telecommuting, managers cannot supervise and evaluate employees based on attendance (a preferred method of supervision).

■ *Need for new policies and procedures:* Not only do telecommuters need to be supervised differently, but their work contracts needs to take into account work-at-home issues.

■ *Start-up costs:* Companies sometimes have to spend money to start a telecommuting program. While telecommuting programs are likely to save money in the long run, a shortsighted company may not take that into consideration.

■ *Security Issues:* In 2006, a U.S. Veteran's Administration analyst had his laptop, and with it information on millions of Americans, stolen from his home. Although the employee wasn't a telecommuter, the incident didn't stop antitelecommuting groups from using this incident to curb telecommuting enthusiasm. Regardless, the incident brought home the need to develop security systems such as disk encryption, digital rights management, and virtual private networks.

■ *Compliance with OSHA, workers' comp, and other employee work environment issues.* In 2000, OSHA amended its statement regarding employer responsibility to check telecommuters' offices, indicating that employers weren't required to make visits to check for safety and that OSHA wasn't likely to make such visits either. However, in a first-of-its-kind decision, the Tennessee Supreme Court ruled in 2007 that employees who telecommute are entitled to workers' compensation benefits if they are injured while working, as long as the injury incurred is work related.

Believe it or not, telecommuting doesn't work for all employees either. The disadvantages to telecommuting for employees are very real and should be considered and addressed before pursuing such a situation. Disadvantages of telecommuting for employees include:

■ *Isolation:* Working at home can be lonely without the social aspects that come from working in an office.
■ *Out of the office loop:* Often, information regarding office events or promotions is passed informally among colleagues. Off-site workers can miss this informal information loop.
■ *Passed over for promotions:* Some telecommuters are viewed as having less commitment to the job and company, and are therefore not considered for promotions.

■ *Jealousy and sabotage:* Not everyone in a company can telecommute, which can lead to hard feelings.

■ *On-call all the time:* Telecommuters live at their office, which sometimes gives employers the idea that they can ask the telecommuter to work any time.

■ *Lack of self-motivation:* Without a supervisor watching, coupled with a plethora of distractions, it is easy to slack off.

■ *Potential to work more hours:* Workaholics are most susceptible to this. When home and office are the same, it is important to set and adhere to home and work hours.

■ *Friends drop by unexpectedly:* Flexibility allows the telecommuter an occasional lunch out, but one must be careful that neighbors and friends don't come calling all the time for socializing or babysitting.

■ *Distractions:* The refrigerator, laundry, children, television, and web surfing are considered by many telecommuters to be the most difficult distractions to avoid while working at home.

Is Telecommuting Right for Your Job?

You may believe your job is not suited to working from home or that your boss would never allow it. While this may be true, it doesn't hurt to explore this type of work arrangement, since it is easier to convert your existing job into a work-at-home situation than to find a new telecommuting job. "Most companies don't hire from the outside for telelcommuters," says Catherine Rosenberry, About.com's mobile office technology expert. "They prefer to use existing employees and allow the privilege of telecommuting."

LAW OF WORK-AT-HOME SUCCESS #8
It's easier to turn your current job into a telecommuting position than to find a new work-at-home job.

Before asking your boss if you can work from home, you need to research and prepare a plan that will show your boss the benefits of a telecommuting work arrangement. The following steps will show you how to evaluate your work situation for telecommuting as well as prepare a winning work-at-home proposal.

Make a list of all the duties related to your job. Be sure to list everything you do, even the stuff not on your job description. Divide this list into "Can be done outside of the office," such as typing, researching, planning, and "Must be done in the office," such as meetings and direct service.

Is your company open to alternative work schedules? Does it offer flexible work options such as job share, part time work, or telecommuting already?

Is your industry embracing alternative work schedules? Do other companies in a similar industry allow employees to work flexible schedules or telecommute? You can find this out through research in your industry's professional organization or through online career and news services.

Even if your company doesn't yet embrace family friendly work schedules, if you believe your job can be done at home, even just part time, prepare a work-at-home proposal.

Preparing a Work-at-Home Proposal

The only way to approach your supervisor about telecommuting is with a written proposal. A written proposal shows you have put thought and planning into the details of working at home. Further, done well, the work-at-home proposal will show how your working at home will solve a problem or save your company money, and all good bosses appreciate that.

Opening Introduction

Educate your employer on the contributions you have made to the company. If you have earned special recognition, increased productivity, or improved the company in any way, highlight it. Don't brag, but be sure that your company understands that you are a valuable asset and have demonstrated that you are a conscientious person deserving of special consideration.

Without giving details of the personal hassles experienced getting to work, give a statement of why you are proposing a new work arrangement. Your reasons should focus on how the proposed work arrangement will improve your work performance or benefit the company. Your boss doesn't care about your child care hassles or long commute. He cares only about the bottom line . . . money.

What's in It for the Boss?

Educate your employer about the benefits of telecommuting, including increased productivity and morale and decreased absenteeism and burnout.

Detail any cost savings your arrangement may provide your employer, such as reduced benefits, decreased wear and tear on office equipment, etc.

Proposed Work Schedule

Describe the days and times you plan to work at home each week. Indicate when you would like to start your new schedule and how long the arrangement will last.

Your Availability

Establish the work hours that you will be available for contact. Provide the methods (phone, fax, e-mail, etc.) that can be used to contact you. Include information on how you will deal with office obligations such as meetings, deadlines, and emergencies.

Job Description

Outline the tasks you will be responsible for while working at home. Detail the duties you will be handling while in the office. Highlight any changes from your current work situation to the telecommuting arrangement.

Equipment

List any equipment or resources you currently have available such as second phone line, computer, manuals, etc. List any equipment you need and indicate whether you or the company will be providing it. As a reminder, money savings is a strong motivator for businesses, so don't expect your boss to agree to buy you a complete new computer system, a Smart Phone with Bluetooth, and a cushy office suite.

Salary and Benefits

If there is a change in your hours or duties, take these into consideration. Your company may already have a policy or you can suggest prorated pay and benefits. If there is no change in your hours or duties, be sure to indicate this as well.

Performance Evaluation

If your duties aren't changing, your method of evaluation shouldn't either. Indicate how your supervisor will know of your work production, such as daily or weekly reports.

If your duties will change, propose how you'll be evaluated. Be sure you're evaluated on measurable tasks such as number of reports completed. Out-of-sight equals not working to many bosses. So find ways to let your boss know that you're as productive or more productive when working at home.

Trial Period

Supervisors may be more willing to grant your work-at-home proposal if you suggest a trial period. It should be enough time for everyone to adjust to the schedule and fix the kinks.

Develop a method for evaluating the success of the work-at-home arrangement. Use measurable tasks such as increased sales or productivity.

Supporting Information

Show your supervisor how working at home has been successful in other companies. Include statistics or articles on telecommuting in your proposal. An easy way to find current news and trends is to use Google's news search. Simply type "telecommute" into the news search engine to find many articles and press releases.

LAW OF WORK-AT-HOME SUCCESS #⑨

Telecommuting is not about you. Work-at-home proposals must always focus on the benefits to your boss and company that telecommuting will provide!

Anticipating and Addressing Employer Questions and Concerns

When my daughter was born, I worked as a social worker for a state government agency. I liked my job, but struggled to balance a challenging baby and work, so I presented my supervisors with a work-at-home proposal. The first two supervisors (who were moms) were supportive of my idea. They knew the quality of work I was doing and how stressful it was to be a mom with an infant and three-year-old. Unfortunately, they couldn't make the final decision to let me telecommute. Instead, the proposal had to be presented to the agency's management team, who wouldn't put it on the schedule for six months.

In the meantime, a third supervisor approached me and expressed concern over my idea, indicating that the agency had to be accountable to the taxpayers. The comment suggested that as a telecommuter, I wouldn't be giving the taxpayers their money's worth, presumably because I would be watching soap operas. This situation highlights just one of the many objections or concerns employers will express.

But don't assume that an objection or concern is an automatic no. There are very real issues that go along with telecommuting and your boss is justified in expressing them. But if you anticipate and address those issues, your boss will be more inclined to let you telecommute. The first step is to gauge the attitude of flexible work options at your workplace:

- Does your company have flexible work options such as part time or flextime work?
- Has anyone worked from home in your office before? If so, what was the response? Was it successful?
- Does your supervisor take advantage of flexible work options?
- How are employees who take advantage of flexible work options treated?

Next, identify problem areas at your work that telecommuting can help fix:

- Is parking an issue?
- Is there enough equipment?
- Do employees share resources such as computers?

Finally, anticipate your supervisor's concerns. Put yourself in his shoes. Think about how your boss will be able to justify your working from home to his boss. Common concerns are:

- *Will your telecommuting cost the company anything?*
- *How will the company know it's getting its money's worth?* This is addressed in the work-at-home proposal in the sections explaining how you can be contacted, what job duties you'll be doing, and how you'll report your progress to your employer.
- *Won't everyone else want to work at home?* While many employees may want to take advantage of working at home, certainly not all will. And some jobs are not conducive to working at home. Your boss may say that since not everyone can work at home it wouldn't be fair to let you. Point out that each job comes with its own duties and perks. Not everyone gets paid the same, often for the same job. Is that fair? Telecommuting can and should be seen as a privilege that some employees can earn.
- *Won't managers be forced to manage you differently?* Your boss can't peek in on you at your workspace; however, in your work-at-home proposal you have informed your boss how you can be reached and how you will be providing reports on your job progress.

Presenting the Work-at-Home Proposal

Telecommuting experts agree that work-at-home proposals are more likely to receive a favorable response if a presentation is made in person. During the meeting, use your proposal as an outline and focus on benefits to your company. Your boss doesn't care about the personal hassles you experience getting to work. Convey to your boss how valuable you are. Don't brag or insinuate quitting, but let him know that replacing you would be costly because of your skills, knowledge, and experience.

Your boss may have lots of reasons why telecommuting won't work. Let her know the research shows that it does work. Show her your research on telecommuting successes of other companies.

Be willing to negotiate with your boss. Maybe your boss doesn't want you to work as indicated in your proposal, but would be willing to allow a different arrangement. By negotiating, you may be able get what you want later, after you've shown how well telecommuting works.

After the meeting, if your boss has concerns, find a way to address them at a later meeting. If your boss says no, don't lose hope. There are many jobs suited to telecommuting. If your boss says yes, congratulations!

The Telecommuting Agreement

Whether you set up an informal or formal telecommuting arrangement, get the agreement in writing. This can protect you in the future if there are questions about the arrangement or your boss moves on and a new boss takes over.

LAW OF WORK-AT-HOME SUCCESS #⑩
Never work at home for a business without a written agreement or contract!

The telecommuting agreement should cover the following:

- The parties involved.
- Days and times you will work at home.
- Date the arrangement will commence.
- Date the arrangement will be evaluated.
- Place (address) of remote office.
- Any equipment the company will be supplying.
- Who will be paying for what expenses (e.g., extra phone lines or equipment).
- Child care arrangements if this is a concern to your employer.
- Duties to be conducted at home.
- Contact information such as phone, fax, e-mail, etc.
- Reporting methods and schedules.
- Any other issues your employer or you may deem relevant.

Plan for Work-at-Home Success

Don't let fear or your belief that your boss won't let you work at home prevent you from doing these exercises.

1. Even if you don't think your boss will let you work at home, evaluate your job, company, and industry for conduciveness to telecommuting.

2. Write a work-at-home proposal.

3. Make an appointment to meet with your boss and present your proposal.

4. Make a list of other companies and industries that can use your job type or job skills.

5. Create a resume and cover letter inquiring about telecommuting work.

CHAPTER SEVEN

Finding Work-at-Home Jobs

WHEN SEARCHING FOR WORK-AT-HOME JOBS, it might seem a bit overwhelming at first. You might not know what you want to do or might feel like you can't find the right job. Ten years ago I had a difficult time finding just one work-at-home job to post on my website. Today I come across hundreds, and handpicked twenty to include in my weekly newsletter. Telecommuting jobs exist, and they are easy to find if you know where and how to look.

There are hundreds of jobs available right now, many of which you're probably qualified to do. But to get them, you have to give up the idea that you'll be able to simply sign up, get work, and receive a check. When it comes to finding a work-at-home job, one of the most important ideas to understand is this: Work-at-home jobs are like any other jobs.

Here's an example of an e-mail I frequently receive in response to jobs I find and post in my newsletter:

dear pajama mama,

i have a computer and can type. i'm a hard worker. Send me more about this job.

I'm sure you can spot the grammar errors that would result in this e-mail going into the delete folder of any potential employer, but can you spot any others? Would you a send an e-mail to employers letting them know you have a computer and can work hard, and then expect to get hired? While that would be nice, I'm sure you know that getting a job doesn't work like that. There is a process that includes finding a job you are qualified to do and applying for that job.

Another problem with this e-mail is that the job seeker has not given any indication of her typing experience. She hasn't told us how fast she can type or even if she has had a typing job in the past. In fact, the errors suggest that she has very little typing skill. A potential employer would disregard her letter because he's looking for someone who has proven she has the skills and experience to type.

I can't stress this point enough: Employers with work-at-home jobs are not looking for anyone who's at home and wants to work. Like their traditional counterparts, they are looking for skilled, experienced employees who can do the job. To get these jobs you must focus on what you have to offer an employer and always present yourself in a professional manner, even if, like me, you're wearing your pajamas.

LAW OF WORK-AT-HOME SUCCESS #⑪
Work-at-home jobs are like traditional jobs; you need skills and experience to get them.

List of Common Work-at-Home Jobs Found Online

The next step will be to match your skills and traits to potential jobs. But before we do that, I want to share a list of some of the most common work-at-home jobs I find when I search for jobs for my weekly newsletter. There is no way I can list every job possibility available to you, as there are too many and new ones are cropping up all the time. But I think this list will give you a good idea of the kinds of work you're likely to find when you start to search for work. You can increase your chances of finding work if you have or are willing to learn the skills needed for these jobs because there are so many of them available right now.

I have also included a list of other jobs that aren't as prevalent as the eight I have outlined, but still can be found on a regular basis.

Copywriting

Don't let the word "writing" scare you. You don't need a degree in English to be a copywriter. In fact, some of the most successful copywriters break many of the rules taught in high school English. The best thing about copywriting is that it can be very lucrative and requires very little education and experience. In fact, many copywriting experts indicate they earned a full time income their first year without having any previous copywriting experience.

Copywriting involves writing promotional materials including ads, brochures, sales letters, press releases, reports, and website content. There are many good books that teach about this type of writing and all indicate that you don't need to be a great writer; you simply need to learn the techniques of promotional writing. Some books that can teach you about copywriting are

The Elements of Copywriting by Gary Blake and Robert Bly and *The Everything Guide to Writing Copy* by Steve Slaunwhite.

Customer service

This is another job that doesn't necessarily require much experience. Most customer service jobs I find are related to order taking and help lines. Usually, customer service employers require you to have a pleasant voice, a second phone line and/or high-speed Internet service, and a headset for your phone.

Sales/telemarketing/research (phone surveys)

Many people hate sales and telemarketing, but if you want to work at home badly enough, it's an area worth trying. Most companies have established scripts and training, so it's easy to jump right in. Like customer service, you'll need good phone skills, a quality phone with headset, and high-speed Internet access. A thick skin wouldn't hurt either.

Transcription

The most common transcription jobs are in medical transcription, which usually ask for at least two years experience. However, legal and business (general) transcription are growing fields as well. Captioning is another growing field, in which transcribers type the closed captioning seen on television.

To be a transcriptionist, you may be required to have special equipment or software. Some companies will supply it, others won't. Beware of any company that requires you to buy its equipment or software. Legitimate companies will provide you with details of what you'll need for the job, but will expect you to obtain it on your own.

Companies that provide transcription services to other businesses are often in need of contract transcriptionists to perform the work. However, jobs can also be found in hospitals, with entrepreneurs (especially professional speakers), and law firms. You can learn medical and legal transcription through correspondence courses. Or become a general transcriber or captioner by teaching yourself and practicing to improve your speed and accuracy.

Translation

The Internet has made the world a smaller place, and many companies want to make their websites, other materials, and customer support accessible to people in other countries. If you are fluent (speaking and writing) in more than one language, there are many companies that need your services.

Graphic or web design and web programming

Often, employers want a combination of design and programming skills. Graphic and web design and programming do require extensive knowledge and frequently specific software. However, many companies will take entry-level employees, so if you have experience, even if it's just a hobby, or you can get the education, you may be able to get a job. Many community colleges offer courses in these areas. You can check online educational resources as well.

Writing

There are many jobs available online and off for articles, blogging, ghostwriting, proofreading, and editing. Most jobs require education and experience, but it doesn't necessarily have to be in English, journalism, or writing. Sometimes an employer prefers that you have knowledge in a specific topic area instead. Still, the ability to string words together coherently is a requirement for writing positions.

Virtual Assistant

If you want to type or do data entry, then the virtual assistant job is for you. Nevertheless, companies hiring virtual assistants do expect you to be able to do more than hunt and peck at the keyboard. Some will want you to be able to type a specific speed and may go so far as to have you take a typing test.

Virtual assistants don't just type though. Many employers want their assistants to check and respond to e-mail, update websites or blogs, submit articles, make phone calls, write ads, and more. The more of these skills you have the better your chances of getting hired.

Many employers will take the time to train you on their systems, but you'll also be expected to have basic writing skills, knowledge and ownership of word processing or other software, high-speed Internet services, and the ability to keep the boss organized.

Currently, most virtual assistant jobs I come across are with entrepreneurs or small offices.

Other Jobs Frequently Found:
- Accounting/CPA
- Auditor
- Bookkeeper
- Claims processor
- Coder
- Data entry (Excel expert)
- Desktop publisher
- Event planner
- Fact checker
- Fundraiser
- Grant writer
- Illustrator

- Indexer
- Mortgage originator or broker
- Notary
- Paralegal assistant
- Public relations/Marketing
- Publicist
- Realtor
- Researcher
- Search engine optimization (SEO)
- Statistician
- Tax preparer
- Teacher/Tutor
- Travel agent
- Verification agent
- Voice-Over talent

This list is not exhaustive. New or unusual job types pop up all the time. But this list can give you a sense of the types of jobs most frequently available to home-based employees.

Can Your Hobby Become Your Job?

Unlike in the traditional work world, in the work-at-home world you can qualify for a job based on knowledge you have gained through hobbies and other experiences. While employers are looking for quality employees, you don't necessarily have to have a degree or years of experience, and in fact, it's possible that a talent or interest you have outside of your professional life can lead you to a work-at-home job. For example, my website, Work-at-Home Success, was initially a hobby, but through it I taught myself basic HTML and web design and was eventually able to get work managing websites.

Putting It all Together

Using the Education and Experience Worksheet from Chapter 2 and the list of jobs on pages 80–81, match what you can do to the types of jobs that are available using the Jobs and Skills Matching Worksheet. As you begin to match jobs to your skills, pay special attention to the duties of your previous jobs and not just to the specific job industries in which you have worked. Remember, duties that you had at one job can be done at another job in a different field. For example, one of my duties as a social worker was to create a newsletter for the families in the program. Through it, I gained skills and experience in writing for newsletters as well as in desktop publishing, and have used them in other fields outside of social work such as real estate.

Directions for the Job and Skills Matching Worksheet

First, pick jobs you believe you currently have the skills and experience to do and list all the skills you have for the job. Once you have done that, go through the job list again and think about some of the duties required for other jobs to see if you can match your skills to more job types. For example, you may not think you qualify to be a writer, but if you have ever written in school, at your job, or as a hobby, there may be work for you. In the Job Title you would put "Writer" and in matching skills you would put "academic writing," "columnist in school newspaper," "weekly blog writing for mom's group," etc. Finally, choose jobs that you may not be qualified to do now, but would be willing to get the necessary training or experience in.

Job and Skills Matching Worksheet Example

Job Title	My Matching Skills/Experience
Virtual Assistant	Type 60 wpm, Worked as administrative assistant, Experience with Word, Excel, PowerPoint
Customer Service	Worked as receptionist, Have phone, Willing to buy headset, Have high-speed Internet access, Enjoy working with people
Copywriter	Basic writing skills, Willing to take courses or get books to learn

By doing these exercises, you now have some idea of the types of jobs you're qualified to do. These are the jobs you should focus on as you begin your job search. Don't worry if the list isn't very long. As you begin your search, you'll discover new job types that aren't on the list or realize you have more skills than you initially thought. See page 91 for a blank worksheet.

Preparing to Job Search Online

Before you can start your job search, let's get organized:

1. Get a binder or a few folders to store your Job Skills Worksheet, scam prevention information, and other worksheets.

2. Consider signing up for and using an alternative e-mail address specifically for your job search. It will help you organize your job search e-mails separately from your personal e-mails. Further, it prevents the opportunists and scam artists from getting your regular e-mail address and filling your mailbox with junk. You can get free e-mail services at many different sites including Yahoo! (*www.yahoo.com*), MSN's Hotmail (*www.msn.com*), and Google's Gmail (*www.google.com*).

3. Establish a schedule for doing your job search. If you don't include your job search in your regular day's activities, you're

less likely to do it at all. Activities to make time for include checking for new job announcements, sending resumes, and following up on contacts. You don't necessarily need to do all these activities each time you sit down to work on getting a home-based job, but you should have an idea of what activities you will be doing each time you sit down.

LAW OF WORK-AT-HOME SUCCESS #⑫
The perfect work-at-home job will not show up suddenly in your e-mail box. Schedule time each day to search for and apply to work-at-home jobs.

Using Job Search Websites

In Appendix A you'll find a list of over 100 websites that list work-at-home jobs. Type the URL of the website into your browser and once the site is loaded, scan the home page to see the different services available. If the site asks you to register, do it. It is usually free and can get you the most complete list of job announcements. Plus some sites will send you e-mail updates of new job announcements based on your search criteria.

Some websites listed in Appendix A list only telecommuting jobs. These sites are easy to navigate by clicking on the job categories in which you're interested. Other websites are general job search sites in which you need to separate the telecommuting jobs from the traditional ones. To find these jobs you need to use the search function. In the search fields use keyword "telecommute" and the other work-at-home keywords following. If possible, leave the other fields ('State' and 'Job type') on "All" and then click the search button. Your search should result in a list of jobs.

If one keyword doesn't yield any results, try another. I generally use "telecommute" as my first choice and "work at home" for my second. Other keywords to try include:

- Contract work
- Freelance work
- Freelance job
- Home-based job
- Home-based work
- Home-based employment
- Telecommuting
- Telework
- Work from home

Remember to only use these keywords from within a job or career search website. Don't use these keywords on major search engines or directories, as doing so will mostly yield business opportunities and scams, not legitimate jobs.

Use quotation marks around phrases such as "work at home" to ensure you get the correct results, or if there is an option to indicate "exact phrase," be sure to mark it.

Take advantage of any services the job search site offers. If it provides a free newsletter, subscribe. They usually provide helpful information on job searching using the web, creating a resume, and more.

If the job site has a job alert service, sign up. When a job that fits your description becomes available, you'll be notified. The only exception is resume posting services. Several of the big job search websites have come under attack for not screening the job offers being sent to people who post their resumes. Many people have lost money to scammers who approached them through the resume posted on the website.

Warning!

Con artists are not beyond posting their scams on job search sites. If you find a job announcement asking for money, it's not a job. Do not send money to these people no matter how tempting it may be. Review the section in Chapter 2 on avoiding scams to keep you and your money safe.

Q: What about fee-based job search websites?
A: "You told me not to pay for a job, but some of the resources in Appendix A ask for money."

This is not as contradictory as it seems. It's true that you don't ever want to pay someone to HIRE you. However, it's acceptable to pay for services that can help you find a job or get hired, such as telecommuting job databases or resume writing help. The difference is that the databases list jobs that are available. It's the same as buying your newspaper to get the classified ads. You still need to beware of scams and choose telecommuting resources carefully. I have visited and use all those listed in Appendix A, so you can feel safe with them. If you're looking for other resources, avoid directories (books with "The List") and resources that say you can stuff envelopes, assemble crafts, and other jobs known to be scams.

Using Other Online Resources

Job search websites are not the only resources for finding work-at-home jobs on the Internet. Here are some other resources you can use to search for work-at-home jobs:

- *Scan online classified ads for jobs;* however, most work-at-home ads will be business opportunities or scams. When reading classified ads, search by the types of jobs or industries that are conducive to working at home, such as "bookkeeper."
- *As you surf the web for work or play,* pay attention to job announcements posted on the sites you visit. Look for links that say "Jobs at XYZ Company" or "Careers." Not all jobs listed on the site will be telecommuting jobs. Usually, the

job announcement will specify whether or not it can be done at home. If not, e-mail the contact person and ask.

Because many companies require at-home employees to live within two hours or less of the company's office, search for jobs posted in your locality. You can do this by searching your town or area on your major search engine. Once you have pulled up a list of websites highlighting your community, look for links related to careers and employment. You'll also find regional job search websites listed in Appendix A.

Plan for Work-at-Home Success

1. Have a copy of your Education and Experience Worksheet and your Job and Skills Matching Worksheet available for review as you conduct your job search.

2. Gather materials you need such as classified ads and the yellow pages if you plan to do an offline job search.

3. Access the job search sites listed in Appendix A and bookmark them on your computer. The websites listed in Appendix A are a simple click away by visiting *www.workathomesuccess.com*.

4. Study the sites and what they have to offer. Sign up for alerts or newsletters.

CHAPTER EIGHT

Getting Hired to Work at Home

YEAH! YOU HAVE FOUND SOME JOBS THAT INTEREST you. But wait! Don't throw your nylons out yet. Once you find the jobs, you have to get hired. How you contact an employer about a job can make or break your success at getting a job.

How to Read a Want Ad

Take out one of your printed job announcements and read it through carefully. Use a pen or highlighter to circle or highlight key points in the announcement. Here's a sample ad to test your skill in identifying important information.

Sample Job Announcement

Virtual Assistant
Part-time position with real estate agent. Must be organized and professional. Ideal candidate will assist agent in:

- Typing and data entry (must type at least 60 wpm)
- Maintaining contact and listing databases
- Keeping blog and website up to date
- E-mail management
- Search engine submission and Internet marketing

Knowledge of Microsoft Word, Excel, and basic HTML is a must. Ability to write clear and concise correspondence is necessary as well. Computer with high-speed Internet access required (no dial-up). Min. high school diploma. Real estate license a plus. E-mail your resume in the body of the e-mail to: Respond to: apply@job

Using the sample above, what words did you circle or highlight as being important bits of information to include in your resume? Did you mark the following?

- Real estate
- Organized
- Typing/data entry (60 wpm)
- Contact database
- Blog/Website
- E-mail
- Search engine optimization and Internet marketing
- Word/Excel/HTML
- Write correspondence
- Computer with high-speed Internet access
- High school diploma

Why does this matter? I know that some of the activities I'm presenting seem like extra work, but trust me when I tell you this little bit of effort can make the difference between living a pajama lifestyle and commuting to work every day. Remember, you're competing with hundreds of other applicants. These strategies will help you tailor your cover letter and resume to each job and have employers hiring you because you're a perfect fit for the job.

Once you have dissected the job announcement, use your Education and Experiences Worksheet to match your skills to the job requirements. As an example, let's say that Julie Job Hunter once had an office assistant job that required her to use Word and Excel. She created a personal blog about cookbooks, and she has the education, typing, and equipment requirements. In her resume, she would highlight her work experience as an office assistant specifically referencing work she did with Word and Excel. Although her blog is a personal activity, it does give her experience in understanding blogs and possibly HTML. Further, if she promotes her blog, she has experience in search engine submission and Internet marketing.

Instead of just listing her experience in her resume and cover letter, Julie needs to match her experience with what the company is looking for:

Don't: "I can type quickly."

Do: "In my current work, I use Word to write professional letters and memos at a rate of 75 words per minute."

Don't: "I have experience using Excel and managing databases."

Do: "I have used Excel to manage contacts and other databases including data merge into Word documents."

Don't: "I have a blog at Blogger."

Do: "I created a blog using Wordpress and basic HTML. I have promoted this blog using ping features, search engine optimization strategies (keywords, meta tags), and other Internet marketing tactics such as search engine submission and article marketing."

Can you see the difference between the two examples? One has the employer saying, "She has all the specific skills and experience I need," while the other is more nebulous. Given the choice, which candidate would you choose?

Hopefully, you can see that tailoring your cover letter and resume can make a positive impression on an employer. So before you send off a generic resume, take some time to match your skills and experience to those the job requires. Use the Job and Skills Matching Worksheet to help you.

LAWS OF WORK-AT-HOME SUCCESS #⑬
Tailor your resume to fit each specific job to which you apply.

Job and Skills Matching Worksheet

Directions: For each job announcement, write the name of the company and job title in the space indicated. Under "Job Requirements," write down the key knowledge or skills you highlighted in the job announcement. Across from each knowledge or skills, write down your corresponding experience.

Job and Skills Matching Worksheet

Company: _____ Job Title: _____

Job Requirements	Matching Skills
Example: Knowledge of blogging	Created blog using Wordpress
Example: Experience Using Word	Used Word to create letters and mail merge

Do Your Research

Ready to write your resume? Tailoring your cover letter and resume isn't just about matching your skills with the job requirements. It also involves matching your skills to the company and industry overall. Some job announcements provide details on the company and the job while others provide very little. Either way, doing a little research on the company before submitting your resume can create an even bigger impact as well as show potential employers that you're resourceful and have research and Internet skills.

Compare the two cover letters below:

Cover Letter A

To Whom It May Concern,
Enclosed is my resume for the job of real estate assistant.
Please let me know if you need more information.
Thank you for your consideration.
Sincerely,
Joanne Job Hunter

Cover Letter B

Mr. Jones
Acme Real Estate
Dear Mr. Jones,
I'm applying for the job of real estate assistant posted at your website on February 12, 2007. Below, please find my resume outlining my skills and experience.

My database experience will be an asset to your business, as I can manage and update your list of real estate clients. I also have experience in developing newsletters and other correspondence that can help you keep in touch with your clients and potential customers.

Please let me know if you need any further information.
Thank you for your consideration.
Sincerely,
Julie Job Hunter

If you were the employer, which letter would you respond to first? While letter A provides a good generic introduction to a resume, letter B offers so much more. Letter B has provided Mr. Jones with information on how Julie Job Hunter can help him in his real estate business. Joanne may have more experience, but Julie has gained the advantage over Joanne because she researched and learned about Mr. Jones's business and how her skills will help him.

To gain the advantage over other applicants, take out the job announcement you found and write down the answers to the following questions:

1. What is the name of the person doing the hiring? This doesn't always appear in a job announcement, so you will need to research or even call the company.

2. What types of products or services does the company offer and how can your skills and experience help the company with its products and services?

3. What types of customers use the company's services? What experiences do you have with this target market?

4. How is the company owned? Is it a sole proprietorship? A corporation? Public? Private?

5. What is the size of the company? How many employees does it have?

6. Who are the company's competitors? What other companies offer similar products and services?

You can use some of this information on your Job and Skills Matching sheet. For example, if the company targets small business owners and you once worked with a company that provided services to small business owners, you'd want to mention this even if the job announcement doesn't specifically ask for this experience.

The best place to start your research is with the company website. The "About" page of a company website offers a great deal of useful information such as the mission statement, history of the company, and past accomplishments. If you aren't able to get the information you need from the company website, e-mail or call the company. Appendix C lists other online resources for researching information about public and private companies.

Calling Protocol

Many job announcements will say, "Do not call about this job." If that's the case, be careful about calling. In my experience, a quick call to get the name of the person in charge of hiring is acceptable, but don't press your luck by trying to gather any additional information. Doing so will only make it look like you can't follow directions and annoy the person on the phone . . . who just may be the one in charge of hiring.

Do What You're Told

You may have ignored your mother when she told you to do what you're told, but when job hunting, ignoring this advice will keep you in pantyhose and commuting to work. One of the biggest complaints of online employers is applicants' failure to follow directions. With the delete button one click away, employers don't waste time on applications that don't adhere to the specifications outlined in the announcement.

Following directions seems like a no-brainer. Why wouldn't you follow the directions the company provides for applying to a job? Too often, in an attempt to be clever or stand out from the crowd, people break the rules and send a resume with fancy font or other materials the company didn't request. The problem is that sending something other than what is requested indicates that you don't know how to follow directions. The result? No job. Companies vary on how they want to receive your application or resume. Some have forms online that you can paste your resume into. Others supply an e-mail address. The one rule that is consistent across the board is to never send your resume as an attachment unless asked to do so.

Some companies will also want samples of your work. Others will want you to take a test. Always do what is asked. Send no more and no less.

The Importance of the Cover Letter

The cover letter is the first thing an employer will read and the key to whether or not your resume will get read. That's a lot of work for a few lines of text. The cover letter or introduction requires a delicate balance of selling yourself without sounding overly conceited. You need to choose your wording and content wisely. In essence, you want to let the employer know in just a few sentences that you are the best candidate for the job.

In the traditional job world, the cover letter is printed on a separate piece of paper than the resume, but sent by e-mail, the cover letter is an introduction to your resume. The only exception is if your resume is sent as an e-mail attachment (remember to *never* do this unless specifically told to). In this situation, the cover letter is in the body of the e-mail while the resume is attached.

There are four parts to the cover letter:

1. Contact information and salutation: At the top of the page, include your name, address, and date. The salutation

should be addressed to a person. Include a title such as Mr., Mrs., Ms., or Dr. Don't refer to the person by their first name.

2. Opening paragraph: Let the hiring personnel know to which position you are applying and where you saw the job announcement. Give a sentence that lets the employer know you have included a resume either in the letter or as an attachment (*only* if the job announcement called for the resume to be sent as an attachment).

3. Brief overview of skills and experience: Highlight the skills and experience you have that meet the job requirements. If you have any skills or experience that exceed the job requirements or have earned any special honors, be sure to indicate that as well.

4. Closing: Your closing should be simple and undemanding. Thank the personnel person for considering your application. Add your closing (e.g., Sincerely) and your name. If you are sending the letter in an e-mail, your name can be directly or one line space below the closing.

Sample Cover Letter

Julie Job Seeker
1111 Oak Lane
City, State, Zip
Date

Mr. Jones, Realtor
XYZ Company
111 Company Lane
City, State, Zip

Dear Mr. Jones,

I am writing in regard to the position of Virtual Assistant advertised on Internet Jobs on January 1, 2007. Below this introduction, please find a copy of my resume outlining my skills and experience.

My Excel database experience will be an asset to your business, as I can manage and update your list of real estate clients. I also have experience in developing newsletters and other correspondence using MS Word that can help you keep in touch with your clients and potential customers.

My other experience includes creating a blog using Wordpress and HTML, and search engine submission and Internet marketing strategies that have over 10,000 people visiting the blog each month.

I appreciate you taking the time to consider my application. Please let me know if you need any further information or documentation.

Sincerely,

Julie Job Seeker

Creating Your Resume

Hurray! You've made it past the delete button and the employer is ready to read your resume. This is another area in which job seekers can easily gain a few extra points by taking the additional time to tailor it to the job. The resume is your best chance for showing a potential employer that you have what it takes to do the job, and can take you to the next step—the interview.

Remember the sample cover letters from Joanne and Julie Job Hunter earlier in this chapter? They illustrated the importance of adding details that are specific to the employer. The same is true of your resume. You want to tailor your resume to each job, focusing on the skills and experiences outlined in the job announcement as well as using bits of information you have learned in your research of the company.

You can use your word processing program to create the resume or your Notepad accessory (in Windows). The advantage to using your word processing program is that it provides grammar and spelling checks. However, if you're using Microsoft Word and will be e-mailing your resume, turn the Smart Quotes feature off, as it will turn your quotes and apostrophes into a series of gobbledygook when pasted as text into an e-mail or online form.

How to Turn Off MS Word's Smart Quotes

MS Word offers a feature that will change regular straight "quotes" into fancier, curlier typographer "quotes." This feature makes your documents look nicer, but when pasted into an e-mail or form, these fancy quotes are transposed into something like this: â€œquotesâ€.

To turn this feature off, in your Word document, click on "Tools" and then "AutoCorrect." Click on the tab that says "Auto format as you type." The first option, "Straight Quotes with Smart Quotes" should be unchecked.

If you have already started your document and don't want to manually replace all your quotes and apostrophes, you can use the "Find and Replace" feature to change your smart quotes. Click on "Edit" in your Word toolbar. Then click on "Replace." Put quote marks (") in the "Find What" and "Replace With" options and click the "Replace All" button. Do the same for apostrophes (').

Note: If you have Word 2007, click on the Microsoft Office Button and then "Word Options." Click on "Proofing" and *then "AutoCorrect Options." Click the "AutoFormat As You Type" tab, and under Replace as you type, select or clear the "Straight quotes" with "smart quotes" check box. Finally, click the "AutoFormat" tab, and under Replace, select or clear the "Straight quotes" with "smart quotes" check box.*

Since the majority of online jobs will request your resume in the body of an e-mail, your resume should be written in plain text without any fancy fonts or formatting. Use Times Roman with a 12-point font. Arial is acceptable as well, but avoid other fonts, as not all e-mail programs read them correctly. If you're snail mailing your resume, you can opt for more formatting; however, less is more when it comes to formatting of a resume. Stick to basic fonts and structure.

If you're ready to write, here are six steps to creating a winning resume:

1. In your text editor or word processing program write your name, address, phone number, and e-mail address at the top of the page. You may want to use a P.O. Box, voice-mail number, and secondary e-mail address to help protect your privacy if you plan to post your resume online. Whatever contact information you provide, be sure that you check it regularly.

2. Indicate the job title or objective. In the previous example, the job title would be Virtual Assistant. If you aren't applying to a specific position, you can leave this out.

3. Next list your work experience. You don't need to list all your work experience, but you should include work experience over the last five years, starting with your most recent job and working your way back. Include the company, job title, years of work, and an outline of your duties and responsibilities.

Remember to describe your work experience with details that fit the job you want.

4. List your education, including any courses you have taken after high school, whether you graduated from the college or not. Don't forget continuing education courses and other classes you have taken, particularly if they will help you meet the requirements of the job. List your most recent courses first. If you don't have very much work experience, you may want to list your education first.

5. Provide other experience you have that might be relevant to the job such as previous jobs not included above, volunteer experience, internships, licenses or certifications, and association memberships. Again, you may not want to list everything. Choose the experiences that match the requirements for the job.

6. Finally, if you have skills, hobbies, interests, or other information that will help you qualify for the job, list those as well.

Many people add a line about references such as "References are available on request." While you should have a list of references prepared, you don't have to make any mention of it on your resume. An employer will ask you for references if he wants them.

As you write your resume, use active words to describe your education and experience. Instead of saying, "I did word processing," say, "I typed 100 words per minute." Don't use too many adjectives and adverbs. Strong active verbs should be enough to convey your point in the minimum of space that resumes require. See the sample resume on the next page.

Sample Resume
Julie Job Hunter
1111 Oak Lane
Town, State 11111
(111) 555-1111
Julie@jobhunter.com

Objective: Virtual Assistant

Experience:
2004–2006   Office Assistant
XYZ Company, City, State
Job Duties: Wrote professional letters and memos using Word. Managed databases using Excel including data merge features into Word. I type 75 words per minute.
2004   Job Title
ABC Co, City, State

Job Duties:
Education
BA College, City, State 1994
Major: English
Other courses: Beginning and Advanced Excel, City Community College, Spring 2001
Other Experience:
Created blog using Wordpress and HTML. Speak fluent Spanish.

Resume Checklist

Before sending your resume and cover letter to a potential employer, check to make sure you have met all the important requirements of a winning resume:

- State only those skills and experiences that fit the specific job.
- Tailor the resume and cover letter to the specific job.
- Use a professional tone.
- Share only the skills you have.
- Share your knowledge, but don't brag or exaggerate.
- Be honest.
- Give only the information the job announcement requests.
- Refer to yourself as "I."
- Have perfect grammar and spelling. Read and reread. Better yet, have someone you trust proof your resume and cover letter for errors.

Be Patient

The one big difference I have noticed between online work-at-home job searches and traditional job searches is that cyber companies often don't respond to applicants. Some companies will indicate in the job announcement that they will not contact you unless they are interested in you. This is a standard rule even by companies that don't say it in their job posts.

While not hearing back regarding your application could mean you failed to apply in the proper fashion or you simply didn't have the skills and experience needed, it could also be the result of other factors. Many job posts remain online long after the company has received enough applications or has hired someone. This is why searching regularly and getting your application in as soon as a job announcement is posted is crucial to your success.

Sometimes you may not hear back from an employer because your resume is lost in cyberspace. Another reason is that the company is overwhelmed with applications and is taking a long time to process them. In this case, it may stop processing applications once it has identified a handful of good prospects. Again, getting your resume in early will help increase your chances of making the cut in this situation.

For these reasons, it is acceptable to follow up, but you have to be careful not to annoy the HR person. If the job announcement has listed a closing or hiring date for the application process, wait a week after that date before e-mailing to follow up. If the job announcement does not offer any information about a hiring timeline, wait a week from the date you submit your resume and then e-mail to inquire about your application. If you still don't hear, wait another week and then call to confirm receipt of your resume and inquire about the next step.

It does happen that you never hear back. This can get discouraging, especially since you don't have feedback about why your resume isn't getting a response. If you are having no luck in getting a response, try the following:

Verify that you have the skills and experience required for the job. Be honest with yourself or find a friend you trust to be honest with you. I have received countless e-mails from people saying they have experience in typing and writing, and yet their e-mails are full of errors that suggest otherwise.

Redo your resume. Focus on using active verbs and highlighting your skills. Consider hiring a professional resume writer to help you.

If you aren't finding many jobs that you are qualified to do, get training in an area in which there are many work-at-home jobs available. As you search, take note of the types of jobs you see often, such as copywriting, website design, or transcription. Take a course at your local community college or online to get the skills you need to qualify for jobs. In Appendix E, you'll find a list of online educational resources to help you increase your skills and marketability.

Never quit. When I first began posting jobs online, I found only one job each month. Today I post twenty-five jobs a week on my blog and another twenty in my newsletter. In my search for those jobs, I find hundreds of jobs in many different areas. The opportunities are out there and expanding all the time, but the only way you'll get one is to keep searching and applying.

The Interview

In online telecommuting, the interview is done either online or by phone. During the interview, remember that employers don't care about your financial difficulties or child-care hassles. Employers are looking for employees that not only have the skills to do the job, but also are committed, energetic, accountable, and productive. Communicate how your skills and experience will meet the employer's needs, not yours.

Prepare answers for regular and obscure questions such as:

- Why are you applying to this job?
- What are your strengths?
- What are your weaknesses?
- Why should you be hired?
- Why did you leave your last job?
- What are your career goals and objectives?
- What do you know about the company?
- How are you a good fit for the company?
- Why do you want to work for the company?
- How do you handle a crisis?
- How do you deal with stress and pressure?
- What equipment do you have to do the job? (Not all employers will supply needed equipment.)
- How much do you want to earn?
- When can you start?

During your interview, be positive about yourself, your previous jobs, and the company. Further, know what you have to offer the company. Remember that you are selling yourself. Work-at-home jobs are not as prevalent as regular jobs, so you need to set yourself apart from the competition. You may be interviewed by phone or judged completely on paper. Either way, make sure that you give a good impression and are prepared to supply any information needed.

Contracts and Legal Stuff

When an offer of employment is extended, celebrate, and then ask for the terms. Getting hired seems like a straightforward deal; however, there are people out there who will take your work and not pay you for it. The best way to protect yourself is with a contract. In fact, never work for anyone without a contract. The contract should outline the following details:

- The parties involved
- What the work entails
- Payment amount and schedule
- Days and times you'll work at home
- Date the arrangement will commence
- Date the arrangement will be evaluated
- Place (address) of remote office
- Any equipment the company will be supplying
- Who will be paying for what expenses (e.g., extra phone lines or equipment)
- A child-care arrangement if this is a concern to your employer
- Contact information such as phone, fax, e-mail, etc.
- Reporting methods and schedules
- Any other issues your employer or you may deem relevant

Work-at-Home Employee Versus Contract Worker

The distinction between an employee and a contract worker is an important one. Not only does it affect the relationship between the company and worker, it can have tax implications as well.

In general, an *employee* is a worker who is hired full or part time, is paid a salary or hourly wage, often receives benefits, and whose employer deducts tax and social security. A *contract worker* differs in that an organization enters into a contract with the worker to complete specific tasks or projects. While contract workers can be hired for full- or part time work, they are paid when certain tasks or projects are completed. Further, the contracting organization pays the worker a straight fee or commission without tax or social security deductions.

With that said, there are exceptions and gray areas in the definitions of employee and contract worker. It is possible that a company can classify you as a contractor, but the IRS sees you as an employee. According the Internal Revenue Service, a business has "the right to control or direct only the result of the work done by an independent contractor, and not the means and methods of accomplishing the result." Basically, when hiring you as a contractor a business can tell you what they want, but not how to do it, whereas a boss can tell you where, how, and why. Since it's possible to have more tax deductions as a contract worker than employee, knowing the distinction and how you're classified is important.

LAWS OF WORK-AT-HOME SUCCESS #⑭
Know your employment status!

Which is better? Both have their advantages and disadvantages. Employee status generally offers the security of a stable job, a regular paycheck, and sometimes benefits. On the other hand, workdays and hours may not be as flexible. Further, employees may be required to work on-site a set number of days per week or month. And frequently, employees need to live within a certain mile or time radius of the company site to attend meetings or other company-related events.

Contract work usually offers the flexibility of setting one's own schedule. Because work is project based, contract workers can work at a tempo that earns them the income they desire; they aren't limited by a set salary or wage. On the other hand, they only earn when they produce.

Another factor in contract work is paying one's own taxes. Often you can deduct expenses such as mileage, supplies, and home-office expenses (assuming the IRS agrees with your contractor status). But depending on how much you make, you may be required to pay estimated taxes quarterly. See Chapter 17 for details on dealing with taxes.

Contractor Tax Benefits

Many people are afraid of paying estimated taxes, but did you know you already pay them? If you're employed, your employer pays them for you every month. As a contractor or business owner, you still need to "pay as you go," but you can do it quarterly. The trick is to estimate your expenses and set aside some of your income for taxes.

Zoning

Even if you're working at home for an employer and not running a home business, you should consult your local zoning department regarding laws about working at home. Some communities absolutely forbid it. Usually it's a precomputer-age policy designed to protect the neighborhood from gaudy business signs, traffic, and business-related noise and toxins. However, many areas now offer a waiver if working at home doesn't disrupt the neighborhood.

If you rent, look over your lease to see if there are any restrictions to working at home. Do the same if you own a condo, live in a co-op, or have a homeowners' association, which have covenants and restrictions. If you don't see clients in your home, work with toxic or unsightly materials, or need to make changes to the outside of your home, it shouldn't be difficult to get approval if necessary.

Plan for Work-at-Home Success

1. Study job announcements and highlight the key skills the employer wants in an employee.

2. Research the company and use the information to your advantage in your cover letter and resume.

3. Follow the directions given by the employer.

4. Create a professional resume and cover letter tailored to the employer's specifications.

5. Prepare answers to common job-interview questions.

6. Learn the difference between a contractor and an employee.

7. Consult a tax expert about your employment status so you can take advantage of tax benefits.

8. Contact your local government, landlord, or homeowners' association regarding zoning for home-based workers. Get a waiver if necessary.

Online Telecommuting Success Profile – Tammy Kipf

Tammy Kipf

Home-Based Customer Service Representative

I decided to work at home so that I could continue my education yet still keep my home. But finding work proved really difficult. I spent YEARS trying to work from home. I tried everything from making jewelry and candles to trying to start a home-based business. What I really wanted, though, was a job. To find work, I used both paid and free job databases online. I also posted my resume everywhere that would take it, although I received more scams and spam than job offers. It took three years, but my persistence paid off when I was hired by a company as a customer service representative.

I love working at home, but it can be hard to stay focused and motivated to sit at the computer to work. To keep me working, I treat my home-based job like a normal job. I log into the company site 10–15 minutes early (just like getting to work early) and I have everything set up in a home office so that I have a professional atmosphere while I work.

My advice to other women who want to work at home is to keep trying and never give up.

Part Three

HOME BUSINESS

CHAPTER NINE

Starting a Home Business

YOU'VE COME A LONG WAY BABY! Indeed, women have made tremendous advances in the working world. Women are CEOs, astronauts, and brain surgeons. And they do it for 29 percent less than their male counterparts, with a child on the hip, and taking care of 61 percent of the housework. While they may not be able to earn the same amount as a man (or even get their husbands to pick up a few more chores), they can earn what they're worth by starting their own business. In fact, women have proven to be expert business owners with a higher success rate (75 percent) than men (67 percent). According to the National Foundation for Women Business owners, two out of three new businesses are women owned. The Small Business Administration reports that since 1983, women make up 83 percent of all new self-employed and over 4.5 million of those businesses are home based! Way to go girl!

Women are uniquely suited to running a home business. They are natural-born multitaskers, able to switch gears from being a CEO to CBW (chief bottle washer) in an instant. Women are extremely busy today, and yet they manage to get most of "it" done. In a home business, she is able not only to get things done, but often she'll have more time to do it.

Home Business Versus Telecommuting

Most women who e-mail me are looking for a quick, simple way to make money from home and believe telecommuting is the answer. However, starting a business can allow women to start earning money sooner and in greater amounts than telecommuting or contract work. In fact, in many ways, starting a home business has more advantages than traditional jobs, including:

- *Doing what you love:* Today more than ever, women are taking their hobbies and passions and turning them into successful home-based ventures. Imagine getting paid to do what you truly love to do!
- *Creating your own work:* Have you ever had a great idea to make your job easier or better, but were rejected by your boss? By owning your own business, you can do the work you want the way you want to do it.
- *Making your own decisions:* You're in charge of the policies and operations.
- *Setting your own hours:* Not a morning person? No problem. Work from noon to 5 P.M., or midnight to 6 A.M. Maybe you need to take breaks during the day to attend to other obligations, or to take a nap. Having your own business allows you the ability to work your peak hours around your already-busy schedule.

■ *Improving the quality of your life:* Loving your job, creating your schedule, and having time for yourself and family makes for stress-free living. A business can also earn you more money, providing greater financial security and means to enhance your life.

■ *Getting paid what you're worth:* Employees almost always make less per hour than self-employed women for the same type of work. For example, as an employed virtual assistant you'll make $8 to $15 per hour, but by running your own virtual assistant business you can get paid $20 to $40 per hour depending on the services you offer.

■ *Creating "job" security:* It's unlikely that you'll fire yourself.

■ *Tax advantages:* Starting a business gives you instant access to a host of deductions.

As wonderful as owning a home business is, it's not without its challenges, including:

■ *Financial risk:* Businesses, even those that don't involve a lot of start-up money, have expenses with no guaranteed return on the money invested. Further, it can take six months to two years to realize a profit.

■ *No Benefits:* It's not that you won't have access to health insurance or retirement benefits when you own a home business; it's that you have to pay for them directly instead of through your employer.

■ *Burnout:* Running the show involves a great deal of physical and mental energy, particularly in the beginning. It's easy to overdo it.

■ *Isolation:* Working at home by yourself can get lonely.

■ *No support:* Unless you start a business through a business opportunity, franchise, or direct-sales, you can be completely on your own. A good mastermind or networking group can help with this, but in general, you carry the weight of your success on your own shoulders.

Top Business Ideas and Trends

The opportunities for starting and running a home business are endless. However, some have greater potential than others. The top business ideas for now and the foreseeable future include:

Products and services for the over-fifty crowd: There are more than 76 million baby boomers with an estimated spending power of over $2 trillion. Current needs are in the areas of health and wellness, retirement planning, in-home care, and travel.

Services for the self-employed: You can start a home business helping other home- or small-business owners. Areas of need include technical support and consulting, professional services such as accounting, and virtual assistance.

Sustaining the future: Being "green" or a "tree hugger" is the in thing. You can be a part of creating a clean world and make money from it as well. Ideas include a clean auditing business (helping businesses and families convert their offices and homes to cleaner products), inventing or creating green products, and selling green products or services.

Health and wellness: Being healthy and active isn't just for the over-fifty crowd. According to Dr. David Katz of the Yale Preventive Medicine Research Center in New Haven, Connecticut, children born in the year 2000 or later are not expected to outlive their parents. The reason? Poor diet. Concerns over obesity and health issues are creating opportunities in fitness and diet and nutrition for all age groups. Other areas of potential business growth are organic foods and products, vitamins and supplements, and health and wellness coaching.

Accessories: Do you own an iPod? Do you have a carrier, a car adapter, and stereo connection for it? People are making fortunes today providing accessories for products such as iPods, cell phones, computers, and more.

Coaching: Coaching was once limited to sports and business. Today you can find life coaches, spiritual coaches, parenting coaches, small business coaches, and more.

More Great Home-Business Ideas

- Advertising
- Association management services
- Author
- Background-check service
- Blogger
- Bookkeeping
- Brand consultant
- Business-plan writer
- Career counselor/coach
- Caretaker
- Caterer
- Child care
- Cleaning services
- Coaching
- Columnist
- Computer consulting
- Computer programmer
- Computer repair
- Copywriter
- Desktop publishing
- Desktop video
- Direct selling/network marketing
- Doula service
- Editorial services
- Elder services

- Environmental engineer/assessor
- Errand services
- Estate-sale services
- Event planning
- Feng shui consultant/decorator
- Financial planner
- Fitness trainer
- Fundraiser
- Game developer
- Gift baskets
- Grant writer
- Handyman
- Home inspector
- Indexer
- Identity thief-prevention services
- Indoor environmental tester
- Information broker
- Information product developer (e-books, CDs, etc.)
- In-home health care
- Internet portal manager
- Interior design/decorator
- Inventor
- Mail order
- Massage therapy
- Medical transcription
- Mobile notary
- Organizer
- Personal chef
- Pet services
- Photography
- Private investigator
- Public relations

- Real estate appraiser
- Referral services
- Relocation services
- Remodeling contractor
- Repair services
- Researcher
- Resume-writing services
- Self-publisher
- Software developer
- Speaker
- Speech writer
- Tax services
- Technical writer
- Transcription service
- Translator/Interpreter
- Travel agent
- Tutor
- Video producer
- Virtual assistant
- Website design
- Web merchant
- Wedding planner
- Writer

Plan for Work-at-Home Success

How many business ideas can you come up with?

1. Look over your list of skills, experiences, and interests and identify some that could be used in a home business.

2. Use the lists of business ideas to help you brainstorm more ideas.

CHAPTER TEN

Creating a Business From Scratch Versus Buying a Home Business

Starting a Home Business from Scratch

Starting a business is not so different from baking a cake: You can assemble all the ingredients yourself and bake it from scratch, you can buy a box that is ready to mix, or you can buy it completely baked and decorated, ready to eat. The same is true of a home business. You can use your own ingenuity and creativity to create it from scratch, you can buy it in a box and mix it up yourself in the form of a business opportunity or a pre-existing business, or you can buy it with all systems set up to go, as in direct-sales or a franchise.

Offering the greatest amount of control and creativity, starting a business from scratch, gives you the opportunity to build something using your unique knowledge, talents, and passion to create the career of your dreams.

The advantages to starting a business from scratch are plenty, including:

■ *Creative control over your product or service* and how you market it.

■ *Administrative control over how you run your business.*

■ *Low start-up.* Often you can start a scratch business with little cash, using sweat equity.

■ *Easy to recoup loss or expenses.* If you change your mind, you can sell your inventory or materials to recoup your expenses.

But starting a business from scratch has a few drawbacks as well, including:

■ *You're 100 percent responsible for everything*, including product or service development, creating marketing materials, and distribution.

■ *You have to create your own systems and plans.*

■ *You may have a longer learning curve as you develop the business side of your project.*

Choosing a Homemade Business Idea

There are several choices to starting a business from scratch. Loral Langemeier, author of *The Millionaire Maker* and *The Millionaire Maker's Guide to Creating a Cash Machine for Life*, suggests that you use something you already know how to do, whether it's from a job or hobby. While this may not result in your dream business to start, it will allow you to learn how to be an entrepreneur by doing something you already know how to do. Not only is taking what you know and turning it into a business easier because you already know how to do the work, but it can be set up and launched more quickly as well.

There are three basic ways to have a home business: sell products, provide services, or sell information.

Creating a Product: Have you created a gizmo or gadget that makes your life easier? Are you crafty in making candles, soaps, or decorative items? Creating a product allows you to use your own ideas and creativity to make money. The downside is the cost of creating the products. And depending on what you create, you may need to consider patents and manufacturing details.

Creating a Service: Selling your skills is a great way to earn what you're worth. While an employer may pay $15 an hour for your work, by selling your service in your business you can charge $25, $50, or more per hour. Services can be sold to individuals or other businesses. A service business is quick and easy to set up. You may even be able to turn your boss into a client. However, like in a job, you only have a set number of hours a day, so your income is limited to how much you can work. One option to overcome this is to expand your services by hiring others to help you provide the service. For example, if you start a tutoring business, you can expand by hiring other tutors.

Selling Information: Instead of creating a product or providing a service, you can teach people how to do it themselves. Are you a Realtor who knows how to stage a home to sell? Instead of selling staging services you can create booklets, videos, and other materials teaching people to do it themselves. Or you can teach other Realtors how to help their clients' stage a home. Information products are easy to create and if you use the Internet, they can be done affordably. However, you need to have a track record proving you know what you're talking about in your trainings and information.

LAWS OF WORK-AT-HOME SUCCESS #⑮
Create a business based on what you already know, do, or enjoy.

Brainstorming Business Ideas

In Chapter 2, I showed you a brainstorming worksheet illustrating how you can turn your talents into jobs or businesses. You're going to use that same chart to further develop your work-at-home ideas. At this point, you don't need to determine all the nitty-gritty details because you don't know if it's something you're ready to do. Instead, you want to develop it enough to figure out if it's worth the time, money, and effort.

Look at the list of home-business ideas you developed in the Plan for Work-at-Home Success in Chapter 2. Pick the two or three ideas that interest you the most. Using the grid below, brainstorm specific businesses you can start in each category—products, services, and information. You may find it helpful to do a keyword search at Google Keyword Search Tool (*https:// adwords.google.com/select/KeywordToolExternal*) to identify subtopics and niche markets for your ideas.

Using the gardening example, a keyword search shows that over the last month users performed over 127,000 searches using more than 80 different variants of gardening including "organic gardening" (14,628 searches), "container gardening" (5,292 searches), all the way down to "nude gardening" (369 searches). Who knew there was such a thing as nude gardening?

Below is a sample Home Business Brainstorming Grid for the topic of gardening and animals.

Home Business Brainstorming Grid Sample

Idea	Service	Product	Information
Gardening	Landscape service	Garden products	Gardening books
Animals	Pet sitting	Pet clothing	How to train dogs book

Now it's your turn to fill in your ideas. You can have more than one idea for a topic and category. For example, in the animal topic I can include fish tank maintenance as a service, organic pet food as a product, and video tapes on becoming a pet whisperer.

Home Business Brainstorming Grid Sample

Idea	Service	Product	Information

Now you should have a few good ideas on scratch businesses you can start. Next, take the most interesting idea and research what it would take to get this business started. To determine if this is the business for you, answer the following questions:

- What materials are needed to start and run this business?
- Where can you get the materials and at what cost?
- How long will it take to create the product or service or information?
- How much can you sell it for?
- Who will buy it?
- Where can you sell it?

Later in this book you learn how to do market research and create a marketing plan that involves many of the above questions as well. At this point, you need just enough information to determine if your idea is worth pursuing.

Once you finish with one topic, consider repeating the exercise with your other ideas. As you move forward, you may find that your initial idea isn't so great after all, and you'll have another idea ready to pursue. Or once you get your business up and running, you may want to go ahead and start another.

Buying a Home Business

Ready to start a business today? Right now? While it's possible to take steps to build a scratch business now, buying a business is one of the fastest ways to get started immediately. Many people prefer the speed, ease, and support that come with investing in an existing business or business opportunity. The advantages to buying a business are plentiful, including:

Brand recognition: Particularly in a franchise, when you buy a business, a part of what you are buying is the brand and name recognition.

Plans and systems in place: Franchises, business opportunities, direct-sales, and even existing businesses all have business plans, marketing plans, and systems in place. You simply need to plug in and do what the plans tell you.

Expert assistance: Part of your purchase includes support and training.

Inventory: Immediate inventory of products or services.

Less risk: Reduced possibility of failure because everything, even customers, is already in place.

But, buying a business isn't the be-all end-all to home business success. There are several disadvantages to buying a business, including:

Cost: Depending on the business you choose, it can cost thousands, even tens of thousands, to buy a business.

Limited control: Franchises, business opportunities, and direct-sales companies have limits to what you can do in advertising and providing services.

Hidden problems: Although you'll do in-depth research, you can't always know the issues faced by the business.

Buying an Existing Business

When buying a business, you still want to start with your interests and talents. Sally Sue Sales may have a multimillion-dollar tutoring business, but if you don't know anything about tutoring or how to run a tutoring business, you'll have a longer learning curve in running the business.

Finding businesses for sale involves leg work. Many people use the classified-ad section of newspapers to sell their business.

Not all these business can be done from home though. You can also find them online, particularly on eBay.

People sell their businesses for a variety of reasons. Perhaps they are retiring. Maybe they're relocating. Maybe they just don't want to do it anymore. And sometimes they are about to go bankrupt. So while buying an existing business offers you the ability to step in and have immediate customers and cash flow, you shouldn't do it without doing a thorough investigation. Use the Buying a Business Worksheet and Checklist below to help you learn the important details about any business.

Buying a Business Worksheet and Checklist

1. Who is the seller? Did he/she start this business? If not, who did?
2. How long has the business been in existence? How long has this seller owned it?
3. Why is it for sale?
4. What is the asking price? How was that price determined?
5. What does the price include?
6. Is there inventory? What's its value?
7. Are the fixtures included?
8. Are the materials included?
9. Does the purchase include use of logos and the brand?
10. Is the customer database included? What is the size and purchase history?
11. Do rights to intellectual property (trademarks, patents, copyrights) transfer?
12. Will the seller provide training and support during the transition?
13. What is the current financial state of the business? Debts? Assets? Accounts receivable?
14. Does the seller work with specific vendors or contractors and will those relationships transfer to you?
15. Is the business required to operate under any laws, franchise or license rules, or other agreements?

16. What is the history and track record? What are the last two years of sales? What are the returns?
17. What current marketing campaigns are running?
18. What is the customer service reputation of the business?

The worksheet is fairly self-explanatory, but I do want to point out a couple of important questions that are crucial to making a good choice. The most important question to answer is what exactly are you getting for your money? If you buy a business but the owner retains the brand name, the patent, and the customers, you essentially have nothing. When buying an existing business, you want all (or all the good stuff anyway) that has made it successful to date. You don't want the seller to start the same business using the name and customer list that you thought you bought.

Further, a business may come with its own set of obligations. It may be in debt or have liens for failed payments. It may have contracts with other businesses for services or materials that you'll need to stick to. So thoroughly research any contracts and debts to which the business is obligated.

Buying a Home-Based Franchise

Buying a business franchise is the equivalent to buying the whole kit and caboodle. Not only do you have a business with a ready-made product or service and marketing plan, but you also get brand name and recognition. When someone invests in a McDonald's franchise, they aren't buying a burger joint; they are buying the golden arches and all that goes with it. The same is true with a home-based franchise.

Buying a franchise has many advantages, such as:

- *Turnkey business:* Everything is already in place. You simply need to plug into the system and do what the manual tells you to do.
- *Brand name and recognition:* People trust brand names, so you'll have a readymade customer base.
- *Ongoing support:* The franchise wants you to be successful and will have people ready to answer your questions to help you.
- *Training:* You won't just get a kit; you'll get full training on what it takes to run a successful franchise business based on the experiences of all its other successful franchisees.

But there are some disadvantages to buying a franchise as well, including:

- *Expense:* Home-based franchises cost $5,000 to $50,000 or more, and often include ongoing franchise fees.
- *Limited to franchise systems, rules, and policies:* You can't put your own spin on how to run your franchise. While turnkey can be as easy as 1-2-3, it can also prevent you from using your own creativity and ideas.
- *Paperwork:* There is lots of it.

There are hundreds if not thousands of home-based business franchises. A few on Entrepreneur's list of top home-based franchises of 2008 include Jani-King, WSI Internet, Coffee News, and Bark Busters Home Dog Training. (You can view the complete list at *www.entrepreneur.com/franchises/rankings/ homebased-115642/2008,.html*). Other resources for home-based franchise opportunities include magazines and books.

Check your local bookstore for magazines such as *Entrepreneur* and *Home Business* that sometimes have special issues on franchising. There are specialty franchise magazines as well.

Just like in buying an existing business, there are many things to research and find out before investing in a franchise. Use the Franchise-Buying Checklist to investigate franchise opportunities.

Franchise-Buying Checklist

1. How long has the franchise been in business?
2. What sort of reputation does it have?
3. What are the complaints and how does the company respond?
4. Are there any lawsuits against the franchise?
5. How many franchise outlets are there?
6. What is the management team's background and experience?
7. What is its financial situation?
8. Do you like the products or services the franchise offers?
9. Are the policies and rules ones that you can live with?
10. How much does it cost to get started?
11. What are ongoing fees, if any?
12. What are other franchisees in a similar territory earning?
13. What do you get for your money?
14. What is the projected income you can make and what is that based on?
15. Have you contacted other franchisees about their experiences with the franchise?
16. How many franchisees have failed and why?
17. What kind of training and support is available?
18. Are you obligated to get your supplies or engage in contracts with specific vendors?
19. What marketing materials are available? Are you limited to using only these resources?
20. Are there financing options?

21. Are there territories? Can you expand in your area if you want to?

22. What are the current trends for this business?

23. What are your options for terminating your contract?

Federal Trade Commission Uniform Franchise Offering Circular

The Federal Trade Commission requires all franchisors to provide a copy of the FTC Uniform Offering Circular (UFC) to potential franchisees. This circular outlines twenty-three items required to help you make an informed decision. Make sure you get a copy of this document and read it carefully before spending your money on a franchise.

Buying a Business Opportunity

Business opportunities are not necessarily as turnkey as franchises, but still are the equivalent to buying a business in a box. Business opportunities take many different forms. In fact, if it's not a franchise or a direct-sales business, it's lumped into the business opportunity category.

Business opportunities can be found in business magazines such as *Home Business Magazine* and *Entrepreneur*. Many are advertised online as well.

Business opportunities offer the same advantages of buying a business that franchises offer. But there is one big disadvantage, and that is they aren't regulated. So, like the other forms of businesses you can buy, you should research business opportunities thoroughly using the Business Opportunity Checklist below:

Business Opportunity Checklist

1. How long has the business opportunity been in business?

2. What sort of reputation does it have?

3. What are the complaints and how does the company respond?

4. Are there any lawsuits?

5. How many dealers, distributors, or licensees are there?

6. What is its financial situation?

7. Do you like the products or services the opportunity offers?
8. Are the policies and rules ones that you can live with?
9. How much does it cost to get started?
10. What are ongoing fees, if any? Are you charged to use any additional services or do you need to order materials to run your business?
11. What are other business opportunities in a similar territory earning?
12. What do you get for your money? What comes in the "kit"?
13. What is the projected income you can make and what is that based on?
14. Have you contacted other business-opportunity owners about their experiences with the opportunity?
15. How many have failed and why?
16. What kind of training and support is available?
17. Are you obligated to get your supplies or engage in contracts with specific vendors?
18. What marketing materials are available? Are you limited to using only these resources?
19. Are there financing options?
20. Are there territories? Can you expand in your area if you want to?
21. What are the current trends for this business?
22. What are your options for getting a refund?

Buying a Direct-Sales Business

Direct sales, and network marketing in particular, has had a rocky history. In fact, no entrepreneurial concept is more misunderstood or demonized. It conjures up frightening terms such as "pyramid," "scam," and even worse, "sales," thereby scaring many people away from a viable home-business option.

But over the last twenty years there has been a shift in attitude toward direct-sales and network marketing that has lessened the stigma of the industry. Today, it's not uncommon for financial experts such as David Bach (the *Finish Rich* series), Robert G. Allen (*Nothing Down* and *Multiple Streams of Income*), and even

Donald Trump to suggest direct-sales and network marketing to their readers. Despite its bad reputation, direct-sales does offer an affordable way to start a business. Plus it provides the products and services, an established marketing system, and personal support.

According to the Direct Sales Association, direct selling is the person-to-person sales of products or services away from a retail vendor. Within direct-sales organizations there are two marketing types: single level and multilevel marketing. The first involves a representative who is paid solely on the products sold to an end user. Multilevel marketing, often referred to as MLM or network marketing, includes compensation for sales made by other representatives a person recruits.

Network Marketing—Maligned and Misunderstood

According to the Direct Selling Association, direct-sales is a $28 billion industry in the United States, and over 74 percent of Americans have bought through a direct distributor. Despite the increasing numbers of direct-sales marketers worldwide, many people maintain old attitudes and misconceptions about network marketing. Here are some common misunderstandings about network marketing:

It's an illegal pyramid. In the pyramid test, the shape of an organization does not determine its legality. If it did, most businesses and organizations, including the government, would be illegal because all have a pyramid structure. What makes a program an illegal pyramid is that there is no product or service and/or people get paid for the act of recruiting alone. Legitimate network-marketing companies offer products or services and income is earned through the movement of these products or services. Members can build an organization; however, income is earned from product sales and not the act of recruiting alone.

Only the guy on top makes money. This is true in illegal pyramid schemes and even in big business, but not in network marketing. Think about this: When will the guy on the assembly line ever work hard enough to become the CEO of the corporation? The reality is that network marketing is the only industry in which the guy on the bottom can make more than the guy on top if he works harder to do so.

Eventually the program will get saturated and fall apart. This is extremely unlikely. First of all, there are 6.5 billion people on the planet, the majority of whom do not have a network-marketing business. Second, every day someone turns eighteen, adding potential new customers and networkers. Third, every day someone is born, adding future networkers to the population. But I think the best argument against the saturation idea is given by Tim Sales in *Zig Ziglar's Network Marketing for Dummies* book. To paraphrase, he asks, "Do you know anyone without a refrigerator? No? That doesn't stop GE from selling them."

It doesn't work. The only time legitimate network marketing doesn't work is when the person doesn't work it. The fact is, network marketing's failure rate isn't any higher than any other business start-up.

No one gets rich and most people fail. The reality is that the 2 to 10 percent of network marketers that make money are also the 2 to 10 percent who really work their business. Further, because it's so easy and inexpensive to get into direct-sales, it's also easier to quit. People do more research when more money is involved, and they are less likely to walk away from a $5,000 investment than a $100 investment. Nevertheless, it is important to point out that getting rich shouldn't be the marker by which network marketing is measured. Many people don't want to get rich. They want to buy a house or stay home with kids or pay off debt. They just want to work a few hours a week and earn a few hundred bucks. Many people like the direct-sales industry because it has:

- Low start-up, usually from $25 to $500.
- Personal support and training.
- A sky-is-the-limit earning potential. While most people don't get rich, the potential is there. I have met a fair share of six-figure network marketers.
- Products and services in place.
- A marketing system and tools.
- Can be worked as many or as few hours as you'd like.

Of course, there are several disadvantages to direct-sales businesses, including:

- You may get a lot of pressure to perform.
- Depending on your sponsor, you may not get the support you want or need.
- There may be limitations on advertising. Some companies won't allow you to use their name in advertising. Others only allow distributors who have reached a certain level to advertise in the Yellow Pages.
- Many prevent you from running another direct-sales business with a different company simultaneously.
- Negative perception in the general population.

Choosing a network-marketing business can be a challenge, as there are so many of them and more every day. Here are some tips to help you:

■ *Choose a company that is at least five years old,* as most companies that fail do so in the first five years.

■ *Check that it's listed with the Direct Selling Association,* *www.dsa.org,* which has strict standards for member companies.

■ *Choose a company with products and services you can get excited about and would really use.* Many people make the mistake of choosing an opportunity based on perceived ease and income. Big mistake. You have to like and know your products if other people are going to believe you when you promote them. Consumable products that people use are usually easier to promote than obscure or expensive products and services.

■ *Understand how you get paid. It should be based on product volume.* Most compensation plans include a percentage payment on products sold by you, overrides on others you help join the business, and bonuses for achieving sales or recruiting milestones.

■ *Run the numbers.* A company that pays only 2 percent on the sale of products should either have a big price tag (which can be hard to sell) or something that is really easy to sell.

■ *Understand the refund policy.* Read it. Know it. Do you get fifteen days to try it out or a year? Do you have to return everything to get your money back? Do you have to write a letter or will it accept an e-mail or fax? You'd be surprised at how many disgruntled former MLMers out there are complaining about not getting a refund, but never actually read the refund policy.

■ *Study the marketing plan.* Talk to your potential sponsor to learn how the company suggests promoting the products and the opportunity. How does your sponsor do it? Many people are part of teams that have set up their own marketing tools and resources, so find out about that as well. For example, a company might promote the one-on-one or party plan, but its members may have online strategies and phone teleconferencing calls that can be used instead. Whatever the plan is, make sure you're willing to do it. If it wants you to build a list of 100 people, do it.

■ *Find a sponsor that you like and feel comfortable working with.* That person is your coach and mentor. Don't be afraid to use them. On the other hand, they won't build your business for you, so do what your sponsor tells you to do.

Ads for direct-sales companies are everywhere, including magazines and online work-at-home resources. However, one of the best places to start is at the Direct Selling Association's website, *www.dsa.org*, where you can search companies by the types of products and services they sell. When you find a company that sounds intriguing, use the Direct-Sales Company Checklist to research it.

Direct-Sales Company Checklist

1. How long has the company been in business?
2. How many distributors are there?
3. How many distributors are in your area? These people are your competition.
4. Who is on the management team and what is its background?
5. What are the complaints and how are they handled? Check the Better Business Bureau in the state the company is headquartered.
6. Are there any lawsuits against the company?
7. Do you like the products and or services? Would you buy them even if you didn't get paid to market them?

8. Do you believe in the products/company enough to share them with others?

9. Is the focus on recruiting or product sales? It should be on product sales.

10. How does the company earn its money? Sale of kits? Product/service sales? It should be on the sales of products or services.

11. What resources and support does the company supply?

12. What resources and support does your sponsor supply?

13. How is the compensation plan structured? Have you run the numbers to see what it would take to earn your goal amount of income?

14. What is the main marketing method? Party plan? One-on-one meetings?

15. What is the financial status of the company?

16. What are your projected earnings? What are they based on? What is the average income? Direct-sales companies are required to provide average earning disclaimers.

17. What are the overrides?

18. Is there sales tax and who collects and pays it?

19. Do you need a business license?

20. Is it recommended that you invest in inventory? How much? Will the company buy it back? Only buy inventory if the company will buy it back if you don't sell it.

21. Are there any quotas for earning your check?

22. How many people fail and why?

23. What does your sponsor require of you?

24. What is the feedback from other members in your sponsor's downline?

25. Can you talk to members of your sponsor's upline?

26. Are you required to invest in motivational tools such as books and tapes? Most companies offer these, but they should not be required.

27. What is the feedback from customers on the product?

28. What is your feeling about the company and the sponsor?

Which Business Option Is Best for You?

From existing businesses and franchises to business opportunities and direct-sales, which business option should you choose? That is something only you can answer. Here are some things to consider as you evaluate each type of business:

Cost: Existing businesses and franchises can be very expensive, whereas business opportunities are less, and direct-sales businesses are generally the least expensive of all.

Control: Buying an existing business will give you more control than buying a franchise. Business opportunities and direct-sales businesses usually have systems in place, but you can still add your own touch, as long as it doesn't violate any of the company's policies.

Training: This can vary depending on the company. Choose one that has extensive training and even more support.

What interests you? There may not be a direct-sales company that involves products or services that interest you. In that case, a business opportunity or existing business may be a better bet.

Before Signing on the Dotted Line

You'd be surprised at the number of people who join or buy a business without reading what they are contractually agreeing to. Many of the complaints I read about businesses are made by people that could have avoided the failure, disappointment, and the feeling of being ripped off if they had read the contract.

When reading the contract, be sure you understand:

- What your investment gets you. Kits? Products?
- The refund policy. How long is it? What's required to get a refund?

- The policies and rules.
- How you get paid. Weekly? Monthly? Direct deposit? Check?
- Any ongoing fees or investments.

LAWS OF WORK-AT-HOME SUCCESS #⑯
Don't sign anything without reading it fully!

Plan for Work-at-Home Success

1. Review what you know, do, and enjoy and brainstorm business ideas.

2. Visit Googles Keyword Tool, *https://adwords.google.com/select/KeywordToolExternal*, to get more ideas based on your general ideas.

3. Use the Home Business Brainstorming Grid to develop your ideas into products, services, or information products.

4. Determine if you'd rather create your business from scratch or buy a business.

5. Research businesses for sale online and in your local paper. Focus on those that fit your knowledge and interests.

6. Research franchises, business opportunities, and direct-sales companies that offer products and services that you are knowledgeable about or enjoy. There are books, magazines, and websites including the Direct Selling Association (*www.dsa.org*) to help you find possible companies.

7. Use the questionnaires for each business type to get the details of any companies that interest you.

8. READ EVERYTHING CAREFULLY! If you're not sure of something, ask questions or have a lawyer check it out.

CHAPTER ELEVEN

Starting a Business Online

THE INTERNET HAS MADE WORK-AT-HOME SUCCESS POSSIBLE. It has allowed us to truly work when and how we want. The Internet has made working at home fast, easy, and affordable and eliminated many of the barriers to working at home such as money and face-to-face sales.

The Internet offers an additional opportunity to expand current home-based businesses and has created new opportunities that hadn't existed before, such as eBay and affiliate marketing. I truly believe that anyone who wants to work at home now can, thanks to the Internet, because it's:

Affordable. For the cost of Internet service, you can reach customers worldwide in an instant with news, sales, and more.

Worldwide. With the Internet you can expand your market from your neighbors to the rest of the world. Even if your market is local, with so many people going to the Internet for information before buying, having a website can help you reach local or nearby areas that you wouldn't have reached otherwise.

Open 24/7. The Internet never sleeps. A website can not only make sales while you're sleeping or running errands, it can disseminate or gather information, any time of the day or night, even on holidays.

Customer friendly. Today, people want information before they buy. Your website can give them everything they need to make an informed decision without leaving home. Further, it can provide hints, tips, sales updates, and more to keep them coming back to you.

There really are no disadvantages to doing business online, but there are some things to consider.

First, you must be comfortable using the computer. While you don't have to be a high-tech person to succeed online, you do have to feel comfortable working with a computer or have a willingness to learn and use one.

Internet businesses aren't as turnkey as many people think. Many online gimmicks make it seem like you can sign up for a program and it will make you money all by itself. That's just not true. Like any other work-at-home endeavor, Internet businesses require work, constant evaluation, and the ability to keep up with new trends.

Finally, if you don't have the necessary equipment already, it can take a hefty investment to get started.

Bringing an Existing Business Online

If you have an existing offline business, consider developing an online presence. In fact, most business experts suggest that if you don't have an online presence, you're missing a big piece of the marketing pie.

Even if your target market is your neighborhood, having a website with your business information will help your neighbors find and learn about you. Plus you can offer e-mailed newsletters and specials, updates on sales, and manage customer service issues.

LAWS OF WORK-AT-HOME SUCCESS #⑰
If your business isn't online, you're missing out on potential customers.

Bringing an existing business online isn't hard. Often, a one-page website or blog is all you need. Or you can create an online storefront with shopping carts and payment processing to go along with your offline business. To bring your business online:

1. Find out if there are existing websites you can tap into. If you're involved in a franchise, business opportunity, or direct-sales company, check to see if the company or other representatives have websites that you can use.

2. Is there an online city directory that you can sign up to use? These cost money, but often have easy website building programs or professionals that will build it for you.

3. Determine what you want the website to do. Will it be a basic one-page site that offers information, contact details, and directions to your location? Or will it also include the ability to buy online? Do you want people to register to receive information, coupons, or a catalog (mailing list)?

4. Who is the target market for your business? Is it limited to your city or will people all across the country, even the world, be able to buy and use your products and services?

5. Are there any limitations to what you can do online? Are there rules in your industry about online marketing? If you are involved in a franchise, business opportunity, or direct-sales company, are there policies governing online marketing and websites? Many companies have rules about whether or not you can use the company's name and how you can market online.

6. Who will build the site? Will you build it or will you hire a service or freelancer?

7. Is your business name available as a domain name? If not, is there something close?

Starting an Online Business from Scratch

Again, starting an online business from scratch isn't much different from starting an offline business from scratch. You still can create or find a product, service, or information to sell. The one difference is that the Internet offers additional resources for making money online, including eBay, Amazon.com, and storefront services, affiliate programs, and advertising sales.

Don't worry if you don't understand what all this means now. The next few chapters will outline how to make money using all these resources. At this point, you simply need to understand that you have many options for making money with your idea using the Internet.

Choosing an Online Business

Back in Chapter 10, you filled out the Home Business Brainstorming Grid. The same ideas you listed in creating an offline business can also be brought online. So if you haven't done the Home Business Brainstorming Grid, go back and do it. If you did do it, pull it out and add any ideas that have come to mind since the last time you referred to it.

Whether you're looking to bring your existing business online, start a business from scratch, or buy a business, use the five steps below to determine if your idea or opportunity is a potential online money maker.

Step One: Is there interest in your topic? The easiest way to find out if people are interested in your topic is by finding out how many searches are done using your topic keywords. This is easily done by visiting *https://adwords.google.com/select/Key wordToolExternal* and typing in your main keyword. We did this before to get new business ideas. This time you want to pay attention to the number of times your keyword was searched in the last month. The more the better.

Step Two: How many other websites are there in your topic area? Type your keyword into your favorite search engine to see how many websites exist using your keyword. Ideally you want a topic that has lots of searches, but few website resources.

Step Three: Who are your competitors? In Step Two you discovered what sites have top ranking in the search engines using your keywords. Click on the top sites to see what they offer. Do they sell products, provide services, or offer information? What kinds of ads are they running? Do they have an e-mail newsletter? If so, sign up to learn about the information they send out. How do they make money? Ads? Affiliate programs? Selling their own products or services? How are they similar and different from your vision so far?

Step Four: What are the current trends for your idea? Is this a fad that will come and go like pet rocks? Is it a trend that will last a short while before petering out such as Beanie Babies? Or does it have a long shelf life?

Step Five: How much can you make? This will depend on what income model you choose. Will you sell products you make and/or use affiliate programs? Do you want to provide a service? Potential income also depends on your skills, not just in being an expert on your topic, but in getting the word out about what you offer.

In Chapter 10 you read the results of a keyword search on "gardening." Using the Home Business Brainstorming Grid, we came up with the following ideas for gardening businesses:

Home Business Brainstorming Grid Sample

Idea	Service	Product	Information
Gardening	Landscape service	Garden products	Gardening books

Based on what you've learned so far, what are some viable online business options? How about web design for gardening websites, gardening consultant, or sales of gardening products through a website or eBay? Other ideas include selling how-to gardening information e-books (downloadable books) through a website or blog or providing free gardening information and monetizing with advertising and affiliate programs. Or you can do any combination of the above.

Home Business Brainstorming Grid Sample Including Online Business Ideas

Idea	Service	Product	Information
Gardening	Landscape service	Garden products	Gardening books
Gardening	Web design for garden website	Garden products on eBay	Gardening e-books
Gardening	Gardening consultant	Product sales through affiliate programs	

Again, it's okay if you don't completely understand eBay or affiliate programs, as you'll be learning more about these and other resources in the next chapters.

Plan for Work-at-Home Success

1. If you have an existing business, research ways to bring it online. Can you sell your products or services online? Can a website help you reach more clients?

2. If you're looking to buy a business, review Chapter 10 and use the checklists to evaluate businesses.

3. Pull out your Home Business Brainstorming Grid and follow the steps to identify viable ideas that you can use to create a business from scratch. Use your research of other websites to gain ideas about online income options in your topic area.

Online Business Success Profile: Angela Wills

Internet Profit Planning
www.MarketersMojo.com

As soon as my son was born I felt a very strong desire to work from home. I had always wanted the freedom of being my own boss, but having a child fueled that motivation enough for me to make it happen.

I knew I wanted to work at home and on the Internet, but it took me a long time to decide what really suited me. I spent a lot of time online going to various work-at-home forums. It quickly became apparent that in order to learn how to make money online I needed to invest in some learning materials. I purchased some courses on Internet marketing and started learning as much as I could. At first I did virtual assistance while I was working my full-time job. When I started learning more about the process of building a web presence and getting people to come to visit a website, I found it fascinating and knew I wanted to do it as a business. Today I run a business that provides marketing services to people who promote a product or service on the Internet.

My start-up costs were minimal. All I really needed to pay for was website hosting, a newsletter service, and that's it. Everything else I needed I already had because I had been on the Internet for a long time and had done lots of research before I started my business. I funded my venture from my full time job earnings. In less than a month I had a full roster of clients who more than paid for my initial investment. I was able to quit my job after working on my business part time for about a year.

I'm very active in marketing my business, since I'm in the business of marketing. Networking and word-of-mouth referrals are the two biggest ways I market my business. Other marketing strategies I use include:

- Writing and submitting articles to relevant directories
- Building an e-mail list
- Being active in forums in my niche
- Ads in targeted newsletters
- Writing on a business blog and guest blogging on other popular blogs

One of the biggest challenges when I started my business was trying to balance work-at-home life with home life. I'm a single mom and I found the lines between work and life were easily blurred when I was working at home. Sometimes it's easy to spend too much time working on your business when you should be spending time with family. To help me, I have someone watch my son while I work. When I'm finished working for the day, that's it and his time with me starts.

My biggest challenge right now is having a steady income. Because I'm hired only when clients need work, my income isn't regular. But I'm taking steps to fix that by taking clients on retainer only or who buy prepaid chunks of time. I also have more assistants as part of my team so we can take on more work.

I would advise any woman who wanted to work at home to get online and start learning about Internet marketing, and watching what other people do. You can learn a lot for free online, but at some point you'll also need to invest in yourself and spend some money. Just make sure it's on worthwhile learning resources.

CHAPTER TWELVE

Making Money with eBay, Amazon.com, and Storefronts

IF YOU HAVE PRODUCTS TO SELL, but don't want the hassle of building a website with shopping carts and payment processing systems, you're in luck. The Internet now has a host of resources that can have you up and selling your wares in a few minutes.

The fastest and easiest way to get started is through eBay or Amazon.com. The advantages of using either of these services include:

- They're free to join.
- You can start small by selling items around the house.
- You can make money quickly . . . within three to seven days.

However, there are a few drawbacks, such as:

- You need to do inventory management.
- There is the hassle of packaging and shipping products.

■ Finding reputable, reliable wholesale products and drop shippers can be a challenge.

■ You will have stiff competition from others. There are over 200 million eBay members worldwide!

■ In auctions, the price is determined by the buyer, so while you can make a lot, you can also end up selling something for much lower than you intended.

Quick-Start Guide to Getting Started on eBay

Many people make a full time income through eBay alone, while others use it as one part of a total marketing plan. Either way, eBay offers an affordable, fast, and easy way to make money online.

The basics involve a "seller" listing an "item" for sale, and potential "buyers" bidding on the item. At the end of the auction term, the last and largest bid wins. The winning buyer pays the seller, and seller packs and ships the product to the buyer. This sounds very straightforward, and it is. However, successful eBayers conduct copious research and use a variety of tools to make sure they have hot items that sell for top price. Top sellers will have tens if not hundreds of items for sale at any given time. All this makes eBay as much of a job in logistics as anything. For that reason, I suggest prospective eBayers take a test drive by selling items around the home. This practice can let you know if you want to deal with all the aspects of selling on eBay. To get started selling on eBay:

1. Find items around the home that you don't want or need.

2. Visit eBay at *www.eBay.com.* Do a search to see if other people are selling the items you have and for how much.

3. Sign up for eBay. Visit *www.eBay.com* and click on "Register."

Fill in the form with your name and contact information, username and password, and read and agree to the fine print. When choosing your eBay username, pick one you don't mind having for a business. Snickerdoodle may be your nickname, but unless you're selling cookies, it isn't a very professional sounding name.

4. Check your e-mail for a registration confirmation. Click on the link in the e-mail to confirm.

5. Go back to *www.eBay.com* and click on "Sign In" using your username and password.

6. Click on "My eBay." This area contains all the information about your account, including your current items for sale, those that have sold, and items you're bidding on or have bought. Through here you can send an invoice to people who win your item, print out an invoice and shipping label, buy and print postage, and much more. At the top of this page you'll see your username and your rating. Each time you sell or buy and get positive feedback on the transaction, you earn a rating point (if you get a neutral rating you earn 0 points, and a negative rating earns -1). As your ratings go up, you earn different-colored stars and prestige.

7. To sell an item, click on "Sell" at the top right of the page. eBay is very intuitive in helping you classify and list your item. Simply enter your item's name in the box and click "Start Selling." eBay will provide a list of possible categories for your item. Or you can click on the "Browse Categories" tab to pick your own.

8. If you stick with the "Search Categories" tab, put a check mark in the category that best fits your item and click "Continue." eBay will ask if you want to list your item in a second category for an additional fee. If you don't want to do that, just click "No Thanks."

9. The next page is where you'll input your item's information. Use the title to give as much information as possible. "Woman's Blue Party Dress" isn't as descriptive as "Woman's Blue *Brand Name* Dress Size 10" (where I said *brand name* is the actual brand of the dress if it's a selling feature). You can add a subtitle for an additional fifty cents if you feel your item needs it.

10. The next section asks for a picture. One picture can be included for free. Additional pictures are fifteen cents. eBay offers additional picture options for a fee. Take a digital picture of your item and upload the picture using the "Add Picture" button.

11. Add a description of your item. eBay allows you to use standard text or HTML in your description. Remember to include all the details, features, and even benefits of your item so buyers know exactly what they're bidding on. You can use eBay themes to make your page fancier for an additional cost. You can also add a counter for free.

12. Indicate the starting amount of the item and the auction length in the next section.

13. eBay now offers members the ability to connect through Skype. (Skype is a software allowing people to make phone calls over the Internet. Calls made to other Skype users are free, while calls to landlines or cell phones are charged a fee.) In this section you can indicate whether or not you want to use Skype or e-mail to communicate with other members.

14. The next section provides details on how you'd like to be paid. Many people pay through PayPal today, although a few will want to send a check. It's recommended that you take a cashier's check over a personal check. If you do take personal checks, wait until the check clears your bank account before you send the item to ensure you aren't being swindled. Indicate in your listing when items will be sent, and if waiting until a check clears indicate that as well in the description and/or in

the "Other things you'd like your buyers to know" section at the bottom.

15. Provide shipping information, including whether or not you'll ship internationally and how much shipping will cost. Most sellers pass this expense on to buyers, but you want to make sure your calculations are accurate. Don't try to make money by overcharging for shipping. eBay offers a shipping calculator to help you estimate shipping charges.

16. The final section lets you provide information on tax (if you need to charge sales tax), return policy, and any other details you want bidders to know about.

17. When you're done, hit the "Continue" button. eBay will give you an overview of your page. You can click "Edit" to make changes. If you're happy with the listing, simply click the "List Item" button.

18. Repeat the listing process again to sell more items.

19. You can track the number of watchers and bids through My eBay. eBay will notify you if potential bidders have questions and give you the results of your auction.

eBay charges an insertion fee of ten cents to $4, depending on the starting price of the item. Additional fees may be added if you add a subhead and other listing features. These extra costs are clearly marked and are optional. The only other cost is a closing fee if your item sells. This fee is 8.75 percent of the item's closing price up to $25. An additional 3.5 percent is charged on the price from $25.01 to $1,000. Items over $1,000 are charged an additional 1.5 percent on the amount above $1,000.

When your auction has ended, contact the buyer immediately. You can send an invoice through My eBay. Give sellers a couple of days to pay, as many people aren't at their computers when the auction is over. Package the item securely and ship immediately after you receive payment. Include an invoice and remind the buyer to submit feedback about you. Don't forget to submit feedback about the buyer.

When a Buyer Doesn't Pay

If you don't hear from a buyer or receive payment, send a second notification through My eBay. If that still fails to get a response, you can file an Unpaid Item Dispute (*http://pages.ebay.com/help/tp/unpaid-item-process.html*). Go through the Dispute Process and if the item isn't paid for by the end, you can relist it when the dispute is closed.

Once you've sold a few items that were lying around your home, you'll have an idea if an eBay business suits you. If it does, you'll need to find a source for products once you run out of things to sell around the house. To find products that will sell well on eBay:

- *Use your own experience.* Did your collection of '80s memorabilia outsell your books? If you had items that sold well, find sources to restock your inventory.
- *Research.* In any business, not just an eBay business, you have to sell something that people want to buy. Just because you can get a great deal on widgets doesn't mean you should buy them for resale. If no one wants widgets, you'll end up with a great deal on widgets filling your garage.
- *Study.* You have found items that may sell well, now you want to study what other eBayers are doing with those items. What keywords are they using? Which listings got the highest bids? Part of success at eBay isn't just a great product, it's great placement and descriptive copy. Find out how your competition is doing and "borrow" from their success.
- *Visit flea markets and thrift stores.* Look for items that your experience and research indicate will sell well.
- *Contact wholesalers and drop shippers about their programs.* Be careful to avoid unscrupulous businesses. Further, don't sell

anything without first buying and checking it out. You can hurt your reputation and business by not knowing your products.

Making Your eBay Listings a Big Success

It's one thing to use eBay to unload unwanted items in your home, it's another to create an income and career from it. Successful eBayers are choosy about what they sell. They do tons of research, use many tools and resources to monitor eBay action, and learn ad-writing strategies to entice people to buy. You will need to learn all this as well. Some tips to get you started on a successful eBay career include:

Sell items that many people want! This is a no-brainer, I know. But it takes research to find out how many other people are selling the same item you have and how many buyers are bidding on them. Ideally, you want to have lots of buyers and little competition. As you grow your business, you may want to invest in an eBay research service such as eBay's Market Place Research (*http://pages.ebay.com/marketplace_research*) or Terapeak (*www .terapeak.com*) that keeps tabs on what's hot and what's not so you can focus on profitable items.

Set a price that gets action. Some experts suggest that a ninety-nine cent starting point can drive up bids more than a higher starting point. But that isn't always the case. Either way, you want your starting bid low enough to attract that first bid. eBay gives you other price-setting options such as setting a reserve price and By It Now. Starting out, you'll want to stick with no reserve, but as you learn the ropes and discover what works best with your products, you can use the other features to see if they can boost your sales.

Determine shipping fees. Most eBayers pass the shipping costs on to the buyers, and many buyers expect to pay for shipping. However, you don't want to make a profit from your shipping fees. eBay offers assistance in determining the shipping costs associated with your product. Let buyers know the cost of shipping, how it will be shipped, and other services such as insurance or delivery confirmation that are available.

Set terms of the sale. How can buyers pay you? Check? PayPal? If they pay by check, when will you ship the item? (Many eBay sellers don't ship items until the check clears the bank). Be clear with buyers on all the terms of the sale. Also outline what, if any, the return policy is. Quality customer service is important to eBay success.

A Picture is worth $. eBay offers stock photos and many drop shippers offer professional photos of their products. However, setting yourself apart from all the other auctions is an important aspect to success on eBay. Taking your own photos is one way to do this. Ideally, you want a picture of your item on a plain background. Adjust the lighting to avoid glare. If your item is a name brand, take pictures of the label or authenticity marks as proof. If your item contains many parts, display all materials so buyers can see what they're getting.

Hook 'em right away. Great advertising starts with a great headline. In the case of eBay, you have fifty-five characters available to attract a buyer. Use your keywords, but also include information such as brand name, size, color, and quality (new, like new, never used, etc.).

Tell 'em what they'll win. Once a buyer clicks on your title, they'll be taken to your auction page. This is where you need to sell, so offer as much detail as possible. You don't need to write an essay, but you do need to highlight the important features and benefits of your item, especially anything that sets your item apart from the others listed. Use bullets to make the description easy to read. Include your shipping and sales terms. Always be positive. If you are concerned about unscrupulous buyers, you can use eBay's Buyer Requirements (in My eBay click on "Preferences" and then "Buyer Requirements") to block certain buyers.

Offer customer service. In most cases, eBay buyers have many choices besides yours. You can increase the odds of your getting the sale by offering professional and helpful customer service. If a buyer e-mails you with questions, always answer quickly and as accurately as possible.

Send an invoice. When a buyer has won the auction, send an invoice right away. When your buyer has paid, package the product with care and ship it immediately. Let the buyer know you have shipped the product and provide tracking information if available. Don't forget to provide feedback about the buyer using eBay's feedback feature. You can remind buyers to do the same for you. If there is a concern, respond to it professionally and as quickly as possible.

Use eBay resources to learn more. eBay has a multitude of tutorials, experts, and other resources designed to help you make the most money possible. Take time to review these resources and learn all that you can.

eBay No-Nos

To keep everyone safe, eBay has a variety of rules and policies you need to adhere to. For example, there are many items that can't be sold on eBay. To learn more about eBay's rules and policies, visit *http://pages.ebay.com/securitycenter/rules_policies.html.*

Other eBay Options

eBay Stores: If eBay is the way for you, consider opening an eBay Store where you can list multiple items in one place. You can also sell items at a fixed price and you can keep items in your store until they sell instead of having an auction deadline.

eBay Stores come with additional fees from $15.95 to $299.95 depending on the subscription level.

To start an eBay store, eBay recommends:

1. Visit eBay, click on "Stores" and "Open Store." You'll need to log in with your username and password.

2. Pick your subscription level.

3. Create a store name that fits your business. You have only thirty-five characters, so choose creatively and carefully.

4. Provide a description of your store.

5. Upload your business logo or graphic, or choose one from eBay's free artwork options.

6. Read the terms and if you agree, click on the "Subscribe" button.

To learn more about setting up an eBay store, visit: *http:// pages.ebay.com/storefronts/start.html*.

eBay's PowerSeller Program: When you have an average of $1,000 each month in sales, and maintain 98 percent positive feedback, eBay will invite you to join the elite PowerSeller group. To keep PowerSeller status, you'll need to maintain or exceed these numbers over a three-month average.

Reseller Marketplace: One of the perks of being a PowerSeller is gaining access to eBay's Reseller Marketplace that allows you to buy items in bulk at wholesale prices. eBay screens merchants in the Reseller Marketplace, so you can be sure that you're working with reputable businesses. But like other aspects of eBay, it works on the auction method, in which you bid on a lot (lot as in a unit containing many items).

Making Amazing Money at Amazon.com

Amazon.com is a great place to sell books, old DVDs, and software when you need quick cash. Like eBay, Amazon.com allows you to sell a variety of items including electronics, cameras, kitchen and housewares, outdoor equipment, musical instruments, toys, and more. Many people like Amazon.com because they can list items faster, provide a set price, and have them appear right next to the new item buyers are looking to buy.

The fastest and easiest way to sell on Amazon.com is through the Marketplace. To list in Amazon.com's Marketplace:

1. Visit Amazon.com. Click on "Sell Your Stuff" on the left-hand navigation area.

2. Search for your book, CD, or other item, or use the ISBN (for books), UPC, (Universal Product Code), or ASIN (Amazon's Standard Identification number) to find the item.

3. Select the condition of your book from the drop-down list.

4. Add a comment about your book. This is where you indicate any marks or defects, or the stellar quality of the item. Click "Continue."

5. Enter the price. At the right side of the screen you'll see that Amazon.com provides information about the new and used prices. It will also let you know how many other people are currently selling the same item. Because I want to sell the item, I always price my item the lowest. However, you'll want to take into consideration the quality of your product. A collectible or never-been-used item is usually worth more than the used price.

6. Indicate how many of the item you have on hand.

7. Tell where the item is located. If you're a member and are logged in, your information will be included here already.

8. Provide shipping details such as if you're willing to provide expedited or international shipping. Amazon.com shows you the shipping credits for each. Click on "Continue."

9. View the details of the listing and if it's okay, click on "Submit your Listing."

10. If you're not a member, Amazon will ask you to register.

11. Once your account is set up, you can log in to add more items and view items that are currently or recently sold. In your account area, set up how you'd like to be paid. Amazon.com provides direct deposit into your bank account or you can get paid in store credit (gift certificates). I like the cash!

12. Amazon charges you nothing until or unless your item sells. The fee is ninety-nine cents plus a percentage of the sold price (6 percent to 15 percent depending on the item) and a variable closing fee. Amazon gives you a shipping credit to cover the cost of mailing your item to the buyer.

13. When an item sells, Amazon will send you a "Sold, Ship Now" e-mail. Log in to your Amazon Seller's account to get the buyer's information. You can print out a shipping label and packing list. Amazon.com expects sellers to ship items within two business days. Buyers should receive their orders within four to fourteen days with standard shipping (or media mail for books) and two to six days with expedited shipping. If you need to refund the buyer for any reason, you can do that from your Seller account as well.

Items will stay on Amazon.com for sixty days, at which time the listing will expire. However, you can relist the item with a click of a button through your Seller account.

Other Amazon.com Options

Pro Merchant Program: The Amazon.com Marketplace is fine for a handful of items, but if you're looking to make the big bucks, you'll need an inventory and a fast and easy way to list products. The Amazon.com Pro Merchant Program is designed for sellers who need an online store to sell many items. Features of the Pro Merchant Program include:

■ Waived ninety-nine cents closing fee from the Marketplace program.
■ Enhanced tools that allow for faster listing and easier management of items.
■ Listings that don't expire.
■ Creation of product pages for items not currently found at Amazon.com.
■ No limit to the number of items listed in your Amazon. com Store.
■ Amazon.com continues to handle the payment process for you, but you're responsible for any returns and refunds.

Fees for opening and maintaining a Pro Merchant account are $39.99 a month, although Amazon.com often runs discounts or special offers for the initial months of your store's operation.

To learn more or to sign up, visit *www.amazonservices .com/promerchant.*

Webstore by Amazon: Webstore is exactly what it says, an opportunity for you to use Amazon.com's systems and tools to run your own online store selling your own products and any of those offered on Amazon.com as well. Webstore offers a variety of features, including:

■ Ability to create multiple stores with one account
■ Easy search-engine optimization tools
■ Add-ons such as reviews, Amazon.com products, Amazon Best Sellers, and more.

- Use of templates
- Ability to customize your store
- Inventory management tools
- Use of Amazon's Associate program to recommend Amazon products and earn referral commission
- Offer special deals or promotions
- Order management tools
- Use of Amazon.com's system that customers know and trust, including Amazon's payment processing, payment fraud protections, and Amazon.com's A–Z guarantee

The fee for Amazon.com's Webstore is $59.95 per month plus a 7 percent referral fee on items that sell. To learn more about Webstore at Amazon.com, visit *www.amazonservices.com/webstore*.

Fulfillment by Amazon: Don't want a garage full of products and the hassle of inventory management? Amazon.com offers fulfillment services to pick, pack, and ship your products for you. Amazon.com's fulfillment program will not only package and ship products you sell through Amazon.com, but also any products you sell elsewhere (e.g., from a different website).

To use the service, you need to:

1. Sign up at *www.amazonservices.com/fulfillment*.
2. Ship your products to Amazon.com.
3. Submit orders made outside of Amazon.com to Amazon.com for shipping. Orders placed through Amazon.com will be handled automatically.
4. Amazon.com packages and ships the products.

Fees for Fulfillment by Amazon.com cover:

■ Storage for products at forty-five cents per cubic foot during the first three quarters and sixty cents for the fourth quarter of the year.

■ Order handling is free for media products sold from the Amazon.com website. It's $1 for nonmedia products sold through Amazon.com.

■ Packing charges vary from fifty cents to $3 depending on the price, number, and size of the units being packed.

■ Shipping weight charges are determined by weight and vary from forty cents to $2 per pound.

■ Shipping methods include media, nonmedia, and over-weight packages and vary depending on whether the items are shipped by standard, two-day, or next-day mail.

To learn more about Amazon.com's fulfillment program, visit *www.amazonservices.com/fulfillment.*

Drop Ship by Amazon: Many people are intrigued by drop-ship programs but need to be aware that many are not reputable. Amazon.com now offers a drop-ship program for all its products. To participate in Amazon.com's drop-ship program:

1. Set up an account at *www.amazonservices.com/dropship.*

2. Add Amazon.com products to your website using easy integration tools.

3. Customers place orders and pay you. When you receive the order, you send the order to Amazon.com electronically.

4. Amazon.com ships the products to your customers. You can even add a custom message to the packing slip.

The best feature of the program is that it's free to join. To learn more, visit *www.amazonservices.com/dropship.*

Like eBay, Amazon.com has its own set of rules and policies dictating what can be sold and how. Be sure to read the Amazon.com terms of service agreement carefully to avoid violating any rules.

LAWS OF WORK-AT-HOME SUCCESS #⑱
Read the terms of service agreement for any company you use to provide services in your business.

Using Storefronts to Create Your Own Shopping Mall or Boutique

If eBay and Amazon.com's storefront features don't meet your needs, there are many other services that can help you set up an online store without learning about shopping cart integration and coding. Before signing up with any service though, determine your needs so you can find the storefront service that will best suit your needs.

There are two ways to get a storefront. One is to have your store hosted on one site with it linked to a shopping cart and payment system. For the brand-new person, however, it will be easier to find a storefront host that will provide everything in one place. These services not only integrate the shopping cart and payment processing, but also provide website templates and building wizards to help you build your site without having to know HTML and other programming languages.

When choosing a storefront, check out the live stores used by clients and the testimonials to get their feedback on the quality of the service. Other features to consider include:

■ Shopping cart that can calculate payments including discounts (if offered), tax, and shipping.

■ Payment processing that integrates with your storefront service. Further, it should offer multiple options so you don't lose customers who don't have a credit or debit card.

■ The ability to expand your product line as your business grows.

■ Electronic delivery if you will sell e-books, audio recordings, or online videos. People who buy digital products expect to receive them as soon as the payment is processed, so choose a storefront processor that manages electronic deliveries.

■ Inventory tools to help you manage your products.

■ Live support services to help you when things go wrong.

■ Security to protect your store and customer information. This is now standard on most systems, but you'll want to understand what kind of security is provided and let your customers know so they don't worry about identity fraud.

■ Marketing tools such as product images, ability to offer special pricing or coupons, contact management (e-mailing customers), and affiliate program set-up are additional features you should consider.

The pricing of storefront services varies depending on the breadth of services. Some charge a monthly fee while others prefer a yearly payment. Some want a percentage of the sale and others charge set-up fees. Comparing services can be like comparing apples and oranges. When evaluating an online store service, use your vision of the store as an example and plug the numbers in. What are your projected average sales per month? Use these figures to calculate the costs for each service. Remember that cheaper isn't always better. Instead, choose a service that offers all that you need as well as room to grow.

While many website hosting services offer storefront features such as "e-commerce" or "shopping carts," as a beginner, you may want to get the all-inclusive features of storefront services such as those provided by:

Yahoo Small Business: Yahoo Small Business offers three different plans depending on the size of your business and your needs. Building a Yahoo storefront is very easy and has many tools to help you create a profitable store. Learn more about Yahoo Small Business at *http://smallbusiness.yahoo.com/ecommerce/*.

Godaddy.com's Quick Shopping Cart: This is an affordable storefront solution. Like Yahoo Small Business, there are a variety of plan levels depending on the number of products you want to sell. Further, it offers one of the most extensive lists of features, especially for the price. Get more information at *https://www.godaddy.com/gdshop/ecommerce/cart.asp?ci=9032*.

Hostaway: Good for the newbie or veteran web mistress, Hostaway offers do-it-yourself or do-it-for-me services in its e-commerce solutions. It provides free application for and integration of a merchant account through Cardservice International. Plan fees vary depending on the size of your store and the features you need. Visit *www.hostaway.com* for details.

Plan for Work-at-Home Success

1. Visit eBay and Amazon.com to learn more about buying and selling through their services.

2. Round up books and other used items around your home that you don't want anymore.

3. Divide your items, selling a few on eBay and a few at Amazon.com to determine which service you like best.

4. For eBay sales, sign up for PayPal at *www.paypal.com*, which is free and will make payment from your buyers easy.

5. If you already have a product business, consider using a storefront service to create an online business with your own design.

6. Consider getting a merchant account to use with your storefront. Find out from the storefront service which merchant account services they work with to make integration easy.

eBay Business Success Profile:
Heidi Marshall and Jenn Cangelosi

Co-Owners Boutique Bargains
www.boutiquebargains.com

We were like many moms who wanted to stay home with our children while still contributing to the family finances. We were both subscribers to BargainBoutique. com and selling on eBay when the owners of the website and e-mail alert services (at that time the services were separate) put the businesses up for sale. We met through the acquisition of the businesses and decided to merge the two services together, forming a business partnership.

Today we operate BoutiqueBargains.com, which specializes in helping moms sell boutique clothing on eBay. We search for great deals on items that have a potential profit for resale and e-mail it to members every business day. It allows our members to focus on selling instead of searching for inventory.

Getting started in the business was a fairly easy task for us because we were already subscribers and knew a great deal about the website and business. We finalized contracts, no-compete clauses, and verified the business income. We also created business and marketing plans.

Now that we've gotten our feet wet in the business, we've begun expanding our marketing efforts. We have changed the website's sales page, added a blog, appeared on Internet talk-radio shows, and developed special reports and audios.

Because we are busy moms, we have a hard time separating work and personal life. We find that staying focused and taking baby steps helps us meet this challenge. Further, we attribute much of our success to support we receive at MomMasterminds.com, a membership site for women entrepreneurs.

Despite the challenges, working at home has met our expectations. It's been a whirlwind of blood, sweat, and tears, but through it all we have learned a great deal. We have so much more in the works that it can only get better.

To other women who'd like to work at home, we suggest that you take it slow and be sure about what you want to do long term. There is no such thing as get rich quick.

CHAPTER THIRTEEN

Making Money with Affiliate Programs

WITH A NAME LIKE AMAZON.COM, it's hard to believe this online retailer was started in the Bellingham, Washington, garage of Jeff Bezos. Amazon.com is a pioneer in many online storefront tactics and strategies. One of its most well known is its Associates Program. Started in July 1996, the Amazon.com Associate Program was designed to reward people who referred new customers to Amazon.com. Other businesses began to see the genius of this concept and started affiliate programs of their own. Instead of paying huge sums of money for advertising or hiring salespeople, businesses simply pay its visitors to refer new customers. Since payment is made only after a sale is made, it's an affordable way to build an army of salespeople. The advantage for you and me is that it's an easy, affordable way to make money without having to develop products or services. Other advantages include:

- It's free to sign up with most merchants.
- You don't need a website although most super affiliates have websites that promote several affiliate products.
- It's easy to do.
- There are millions of affiliate products covering as many different topics. If you're interested in a topic, there's an affiliate program that sells it.

Like everything else, affiliate marketing has its downsides, too, such as:

- Over time, affiliate marketing has become more complex.
- Signing up for a program isn't enough. You have to learn how to market and compete with millions of other affiliate marketers promoting the same products.
- Not all products are worth promoting.
- Not all merchants operate with the affiliate's needs in mind. Some merchants don't pay, "lose" data in the system, and even hijack your referrals.

How Affiliate Marketers Are Paid

Affiliate merchants provide one or several methods of payment structure. The most common are:

- Pay Per Click: You don't see this option very much anymore except with contextual advertising such as Google's AdSense program.
- Pay Per Sale: The highest affiliate payouts tend to be from programs that pay a flat fee or percentage of each sale.
- Pay Per Lead: These programs don't pay as much as pay-per-sale programs, usually only twenty-five cents to $2 per action, but they tend to do well because the action is

usually registration for a free offer. People like free stuff and will usually sign up.

- Pay Per Impression: Like cost per click, this is an option not seen much anymore.

Finding Money-Making Affiliate Programs

Affiliate programs are everywhere. The quickest way to find suitable programs in your topic area is to use affiliate networks and directories. Affiliate networks act as a middleman between merchants and affiliate marketers. Merchants "hire" affiliate networks to manage all aspects of the program, including the sign-up of affiliates, creating affiliate links, tracking statistics, and sending payments to affiliates.

Affiliate networks are a good place for affiliates to find merchants because you can browse, sign up for, and manage thousands of programs in one place. Because the merchants have to give a sizable amount of money to the network for affiliate payments, there is less risk that you won't get paid.

Well-known affiliate networks include Commission Junction (*www.commissionjunction.com*) and LinkShare (*www.linkshare .com*). You can find more in Appendix B.

Like affiliate networks, affiliate directories list thousands of programs; however, directories only list and on occasion rate programs. When you find a program that seems interesting, you're directed to the affiliate merchant site to apply. There is no middleman helping you manage your programs or controlling statistics and payments.

Another option for finding affiliate programs is through merchants who run their own programs. If there is a product or service you love, visit the website and search for a link that says "Affiliates" to get the details. The only disadvantage of working directly with a merchant is that you need to trust it to pay you.

My experience overall has been good, but I have had at least two merchants fail to pay what I was owed. So research carefully.

Choosing Affiliate Products/Programs

Just like choosing your business idea involves utilizing your knowledge, skills, and interests, so too does choosing affiliate programs. If you love gardening, find affiliate programs in gardening. If you're an expert bargain hunter, find affiliate programs promoting coupons and bargains. There are thousands if not millions of affiliate programs and the odds are pretty good that whatever business idea you have, there is an affiliate program to complement it.

But don't sign up for any ol' program that appears to pay the most. Consider the quality and reputation of the company and the product. Affiliate programs are most successful if people trust your expertise. Therefore, your credibility is on the line, and if you choose lousy products or work with questionable companies, your online reputation can be ruined. Overcoming a bad reputation online is very difficult, as anything that is posted online is there forever.

When choosing an affiliate program, consider the following:

1. Is the product or service relevant to your website? If you have a gardening site, promoting auto detailing doesn't make sense.

2. Is the company reputable?

3. Is the product or service priced right? Would you pay the price being asked?

4. Have you used the product or service? Can you attest to its quality?

Remember, if you recommend it or have it on your website, you're essentially saying, "This is a good product."

5. Does the company offer excellent customer service? Even after the sale, your credibility can be ruined if someone you referred to a company receives substandard service.

6. Does it have a professional-looking website? Websites don't need bells and whistles, but they should be organized, orderly, clear, and professional.

7. Does it have an affiliate agreement? What are the conditions? What are the restrictions? Read the terms and conditions carefully. Many don't allow e-mail advertising. Some don't allow you to buy pay-per-click ads using specific keywords.

8. How is payment determined (pay-per-action, etc.)? Is it recurring, one-time, or residual? Some programs may have several payment levels. For example, Monster.com has pay-per-action for website registration and a pay-per-sale for sales of the resume service. Some companies offer ongoing services (e.g., monthly services), for which they pay affiliates ongoing income called residual income. Some even pay you if you refer other affiliate marketers in what's called a two-tier program.

9. When and how does it pay? Does the program pay monthly or bi-monthly? Do your earnings need to reach a specific amount before you're paid? Will you get a check in the mail or a direct deposit into your bank account?

10. How does it track commissions? In real time? Can you access your statistics and see exactly what's going on, such as how many people have clicked your link or how many have taken action? If cookies are used, how long are they set? (A cookie is a bit of code that tracks the person who used your affiliate link. If she doesn't buy the first time, but comes back later through a different method, the cookie will ensure you get credit for the sale.)

11. Does it have marketing tools? You only make money in affiliate programs when you refer others to sign up or buy a merchant's

goods and services. Good merchants will have tools to help you do this, including banners, buttons, and sample ads.

How to Join Affiliate Programs

Joining affiliate programs is straightforward. If you join through a network, you'll need to provide information about your website and then begin the process of searching for compatible programs. Often you can join several programs with a single click. When using directories or signing up through the merchant directly, you'll fill out a form with your contact and website information.

When you click the "Join" button, you'll usually be asked to accept the terms and conditions of the programs. Some will approve you off the bat; others will want to visit your website. Like you, they want to make sure they are a good fit with what you offer. That means the topic of your site should be relevant to what the merchant is offering.

What If You Don't Have a Website?

As an affiliate marketer, you are given a special link that tracks you as the referrer. When a customer clicks on your affiliate link, they are taken to the merchant's website where they can learn more about the products and services. While many affiliate marketers post affiliate links on their websites, you don't have to have a website to be an affiliate marketer. Instead, you can market affiliate products by:

E-mail: If you have an e-mail list of customers or friends, you can send your affiliate link and a blurb about the product in an e-mail. Be careful not to spam. Only send e-mail to people who have requested to hear from you.

Pay-per-click advertising: Programs such as Google's AdWords program allow you to submit ads that the service will run on its search engine's results pages and feed onto websites. This is an extremely effective way to market, but it can also make you broke. Read Chapter 22 on online marketing to learn more about this marketing strategy.

Signature lines: Signature lines are your online signature posted in your e-mails, social networking comments, and on discussion boards. Many places allow you to put a little advertising blurb with a link in your signature.

Business cards, fliers, handouts, etc.: You can print affiliate links onto materials you give out to friends and family. The only difficulty with this is that some affiliate links are really long and filled with numbers and letters that make no sense.

Not all affiliate programs will approve you without a website or proof that you have a ready market for its products. But many will. With an affiliate link, you have your own website sales page on any product or service of your choosing.

Avoiding Bad Affiliate Merchants

As I mentioned before, my affiliate marketing experiences have for the most part been very good. But a few times I have run into merchants who don't want to or can't pay me. There are several ways affiliate merchants can negatively affect your earnings, including:

■ *Failing to pay you:* I've had two merchants in ten years of affiliate marketing not pay income I earned. One of these companies was a consumer protection site. Imagine being ripped off by a consumer protection agency!

■ *Failing to track affiliate IDs:* When your referrals click on your link, you have an affiliate ID that indicates you are the person who sent the referral. Most vendors use tracking codes and cookies to keep track of affiliate referral IDs. However, some sites lose the tracking code if the referral clicks on other links within the site.

■ *Providing alternate payment options that don't track affiliate IDs.* My most recent adventure in affiliate rip-offs involved an affiliate program that offered an alternative payment method that didn't track referrals. The result was that I was sending referrals who were buying, but I wasn't getting credit (or payment).

To protect yourself from bad affiliate merchants, research sites carefully before signing up. Ideally, pick a company that runs its program through a reputable network like Commission Junction or LinkShare, which require that monies paid to affiliates to be escrowed into an account.

Further, test your links. When you sign up, click your link to see where it goes. Check that the "Buy Now" button tracks your affiliate ID. Visit other pages on the site and then click the "Buy Now" button to make sure it still tracks your ID.

You also want to track your program's results. Check your website's exit logs to see how many people are leaving your site through your affiliate link. Or use a click-tracking code to monitor the number of times the link is clicked. Also, view your sales and determine if the number of sales seems reasonable for the number of clicks. If things don't look right, visit the merchant site to determine why. Is it a poorly written sales page that doesn't convert well or is your tracking code being lost?

Making Money with Contextual-Ad Feeds

This is really a form of paid advertising, in that you are paid to run other people's ads on your site. However, it works by signing up with an ad system that then feeds ads onto your website and then pays you each time someone clicks on an ad (like pay-per-click affiliate marketing). Google's AdSense program is the most well known, but there are others such as Yahoo's Publisher Network. These services "feed" ads that match the keyword content on your web page. If your website is about gardening, the service will feed ads for gardening products and services.

The contextual-ad programs use calculus and probably quantum physics to create formulas that no one could ever figure out to determine how much to pay you for each click. We do know that most people who buy contextual advertising pay anywhere from five cents to $5 or even more for each click. But that's not what you get paid. Not only that, but in the case of Google, there are rules about deciphering the payment formula. It doesn't even allow me to share how much I make with this advertising. I can tell you that there are people making as much as $600 a day. Of course, these results are not typical. In fact, I don't know the typical income from contextual advertising. But I personally know many people who make $750 to $3,000 a month with these programs. Since it's free to sign up, there's no reason not to try it.

To run contextual ads on your site:

1. Visit sites that offer contextual ads and sign up. It's free.
2. Read the terms of service carefully and follow the rules. For example, it's a big no-no for you to click on the ads on your website or to ask your visitors, family, or friends to click on your links. Your account can be terminated without question or recourse, so read the rules carefully.

3. Read through the instruction for posting ads on your website. Most programs have thorough explanations on how to best use the program.

4. Choose the format that you'd like the ads to appear, including size, shape, and colors.

5. Paste the code onto your web pages. The system will give you a snippet of code that you copy and paste onto your web page where you want the ads to appear.

For more information, visit:

Google AdSense *www.google.com* (click on "Advertising Programs")

Yahoo's Publisher Network *http://publisher.yahoo.com.*

LAWS OF WORK-AT-HOME SUCCESS #⑲

Read each affiliate program's terms of service and marketing policies. Many have restrictions that can result in your termination from the program if you violate them.

Plan for Work-at-Home Success

1. Study other websites to see how they use affiliate programs and contextual advertising.

2. Visit CommissionJunction.com, Clickbank.com, and other affiliate resources to find products and services that fit your business idea. Appendix B lists more resources.

3. When you find programs that fit the bill, sign up and add the links to your website.

Affiliate Marketer Success Profile: Nell Taliercio
Just Online Jobs
www.JustOnlineJobs.com

I began searching for a way to work at home long before I had children, but I wasn't sure if there was really a legitimate way to do it. Since I didn't know what was available, I did like many other work-at-home wannabes do and typed "work-at-home" and "typing at home" into a search engine. As you can imagine, I found a lot of junk and scams. However, I did find a few legitimate work-at-home jobs, which I did off and on for a while.

While having a work-at-home job was nice, I wanted to be home full time and felt that being my own boss was a better option. I researched business options, but when I found out I was pregnant with my first child, I put my goals into overdrive. I knew what I wanted to do, which was to make money from information websites. What I had to figure out was how to make it successful.

I decided to get some help and joined a woman's mastermind group, where I found coaching, resources, step-by-step help, and networking to help me become a successful affiliate marketer. But I knew that having a website in and of itself wasn't going to make money, so I developed a marketing plan that includes a variety of marketing tactics such as:

- Article marketing
- Networking
- Sales pages (for my products)
- Affiliate program (for my products)

- PPC
- Newsletter ads

The start-up costs for my business were low and included website hosting, domain-name purchase, and hiring someone to create graphics. The rest of my investment was sweat equity that involved writing all my own materials, answering e-mail, and all the other aspects to running a website. But I wouldn't recommend that anyone start the way I did. Writing and web design aren't my forte, and so my sites weren't as professional as they could have been.

I started my first website in 2003, but didn't really get serious about making it a success until 2004. By November 2004, I quit my job to stay home full time. Getting a mentor and joining a mastermind group was really the turning point for me. I've found that hooking up with successful people who do the same thing I do has been the most important aspect to my success. Whether it's a group mentoring or one-on-one coaching, I highly recommend taking advantage of the insight of others who are successful.

I had many challenges during my start-up days. I found it difficult to find legitimate jobs and honest information about working at home. As I started working at home, balancing work and family became more difficult. I've gotten through the challenges mostly by trial and error. The truth is, balancing work and family is still difficult. I enjoy my work and struggle with the urge to work more hours than I should. To help me with this, I outsource work to a team of writers, virtual assistants, and designers. This allows me to focus on money-making tasks that

I squeeze in during my kids' naps, before they get up, or after they go to sleep.

Despite the challenges, working at home has far exceeded my expectations. When I first started working at home, my goal was to help pay a few bills. Today, I'm home full time with two boys, making more money than I ever have, and enjoying every minute of it!

To other women who want to work at home, I suggest that you find a mentor. Also do what you love, and set goals that match your values. Finally, be realistic about what it takes to succeed. You aren't going to find success right from the start. You won't be making a full time living right off the bat. A business takes time, and usually a lot of it, before it's making money and running smoothly.

Nell is also an advocate of investing financially in your business, including using paid web-hosting services and outsourcing to professionals. And finally, she recommends ongoing education in the areas of business success and to apply what is learned to build a strong, solid, profitable business.

CHAPTER FOURTEEN

Making Money from Information

PEOPLE HAVE BEEN MAKING MILLIONS WITH INFORMA-TION for many years. If you've ever bought a booklet, report, or an audio training program through mail order or online, you have bought an information product. While information products can be sold offline (usually through mail order), the Internet has made the creation and sales of information products faster, easier, and more affordable than ever. The advantages to becoming an information entrepreneur include:

- Products are easy to create.
- They are affordable to create, market, and distribute.
- Low overhead means you keep most of the profits.

The only real disadvantage to an information-product business is finding the creativity and time to create a product and setting up the online sales system. But even these challenges are easily overcome.

What Is an Information Product?

Information products come in a variety of forms and include anything from books and reports to audio recordings and video trainings and more. Below is a list of common information-product formats:

- Books
- E-books (electronic books)
- Reports
- Manuals
- Home study courses
- Seminars
- Seminar transcripts
- Audio recordings
- Videos
- Training materials

All these products can be sold in hard (tangible) or digital (Internet) copy. Further, they can be marketed in a variety of ways, including single sale, continuity programs (e.g., book-of-the-month), memberships, or kits.

While you may not think you are knowledgeable enough about a topic to create an information product, I urge you to reconsider. As we discovered early in the book through your Education and Experience Worksheet, you know lots of stuff. Further, the ease and affordability of creating information products, coupled with the potential earnings, make this an idea worth considering. Successful information-product entrepreneurs sell their e-books for $39.99 to $199.00, and other products for as much as $1,500. By using the Internet, overhead expenses are quite low, allowing you to keep most of your earnings. Are you convinced yet?

LAWS OF WORK-AT-HOME SUCCESS #⃝20
Everyone knows enough about a topic that someone else is willing to pay to know more about.

Creating an Information Product

Many people get easily overwhelmed at the idea of writing a book, audio course, or other information product. Do I really know enough that people will pay me for it? Can I write or speak well enough to make a quality product? How do I organize all the information? And so on. As Richard Dreyfuss explained to Bill Murray in *What About Bob?*, take baby steps. Don't sit down and expect your product to be ready to go that same day. Instead, take your time. Organize your thoughts. Plot out your ideas. Write. Revise. And pretty soon, you've got something worth selling. Here are my tips for putting together a saleable information product.

1. Start with a written product such as a report or e-book. These are the easiest to produce.

2. Select an idea from your list and do the research outlined in Chapter 11, such as determining how many people do a search on that topic, the number of websites that cover the topic, and what the top websites offer.

3. Use the keyword list from Google Keyword Search Tool to come up with other ideas in niche markets.

4. Make a list of possible ideas focusing on small targeted topics. Instead of a gardening book or audio training, focus on container gardening.

5. Make a list of everything your target market needs to know about your topic. Start with general ideas. For example, when I started this book, my major topic ideas were 1) The Reality

of Working at Home; 2) Getting Started; 3) Finding Work-at-Home Jobs; and 4) Starting a Home Business.

6. Within each major category of your topic, list the specifics readers need to know. Using this book again, under the Finding Work-at-Home Jobs I put inventorying skills and experience, how to find jobs, writing winning resumes, and avoiding scams.

7. Organize your list and flesh out the concepts with sentences. Use headings and bullets to keep your thoughts in order and your writing on the topic.

8. Read your document for clarity as well as spelling and grammatical errors.

9. Have a friend, or better yet a mentor, read the product to offer feedback.

10. Create a website.

11. Sign up for a payment processor such as PayPal or Clickbank.

12. Build a website with a sales page for your e-book or report.

13. Add e-mail capturing, such as offering a free e-mailed newsletter.

14. Upload your website with links to payment processing and book delivery.

15. Market your website.

16. Do it again either by expanding on your current topic with audio or video trainings or creating a product about an entirely different product.

Easy and Affordable Payment Processing

Order processing is easy through PayPal (*www.paypal.com*), or if you have digital products and want to allow other people to sell your product as well (as affiliate marketers), use Clickbank's merchant program (*www.clickbank.com/sell_products.html*).

Making the Product

My first information product was a booklet that told people how to find work-at-home jobs. It was printed on regular white copy paper, with a blue card-stock cover, and black comb binding. Obviously, getting it to the customer required the U.S. Postal Service.

Internet commerce wasn't any easier at that time, either. Only the big guys (like Amazon.com) had payment systems. Little one-person businesses like me had to wait for checks to come in the mail. Later, I was able to get a merchant account, but even then most customers printed the order form and mailed it to me with their credit card information.

Today, technology has changed everything. I can write a report in my word processor, convert it to a PDF format, upload it to the Internet, and have it delivered as soon as a customer pays for it. Further, customers can pay using PayPal or other forms of payment, including online checking. It's all done instantaneously. Further, once I have it set up, I don't have to do anything else. I don't have to process the payment or send the order. It's all done automatically.

Technology has not only made selling information products faster and more affordable, but creating them is a breeze as well. Whether you want to create an e-book, audios, or videos, it can all be done from your computer. Here's how:

E-books, e-reports, e-manuals, and any other e-related document: There are a variety of e-book formats, but most experts suggest using PDF, as most computers (Macs included) can open and view them. You can use the converting service at Adobe.com or buy a PDF converter software. For the most features, including piracy protection, consider buying Adobe Acrobat. It's not cheap, but if you're going to be an information entrepreneur, it will be a good investment.

Online audios: This, too, is amazingly easy. The computer you have right now, assuming it's not too old, has all the equipment you need to create audio files, such as a microphone input plug and audio-capture software (e.g., Windows Sound Recorder found in the Accessories Folder). All you need is a microphone and you're ready to go. For best sound quality, choose a good headphone and consider downloading Audacity audio recording and editing software (it's free) at *http://audacity.sourceforge.net*. Once your audio is edited you can upload to your web server or use a service such as Audio Acrobat or Audio Generator. These services are not free, but they have a host of great features that make them worthwhile if audio production will be a regular staple of your business.

Video products: Admittedly, I don't have much experience in this except for making my family's end-of-the-year DVD. However, video tutorials and information courses are very popular. Some people, like Rosie O'Donnell, use a web cam to capture video. If you're planning to sell your video, you'll want to use a high-quality video camera to film your training or information. You can edit your video online using video-editing software.

Books, manuals, courses, and other printed materials: The growth of print-on-demand services has made creating books and other documents very affordable. Lulu.com offers a variety of printing services and even a storefront from which you can sell your printed documents.

Audio CDs and Video DVDs: In the old days, information marketers with audio or video had to go into a studio to make a quality recording and then outsource the creation of the cassette and video tapes (do you remember those?). Today, you can do it all from your computer. You can make your audio and video and then copy (burn it) to a CD or DVD. Fast. Easy. Cheap!

Plan for Work-at-Home Success

1. Study information products you have bought in the past, whether they're online e-books or e-mail courses or printed products.

2. Take an idea from your Home Business Brainstorming Grid and list everything you know or that someone should know about that topic.

3. Organize the list and provide more detail to each item.

4. If you don't feel you have enough information, interview others in the field. You can record the interview for an audio product and or have it transcribed into written form for a book or report.

5. Determine the type of product you want: a book, report, or audio.

6. Create your website, including sales copy, e-mail capture, and order processing.

7. Create another product.

CHAPTER FIFTEEN

Getting Online

SO FAR WE'VE TALKED ABOUT DIFFERENT WAYS TO MAKE MONEY ONLINE, but not too much about what it takes to get online. To many people, the idea of building a website with all the coding and programming is a daunting task. The good news is that you don't have to know anything about building a website to start making money online. In fact, you can build an online business without a traditional website. Online resources such as blogs, eBay, and storefront services can have you online selling your products and services in minutes. However, depending on your business idea, some options may work better than others.

Websites offer the most control of your web presence. You can create a site with the sights and sounds of your choice. If you don't have programming skills, you can hire someone, or use a template to build a site. Further, there are many free and paid scripts that can enhance your site with features such as discussion boards, newsletters, and interactive activities.

Blogs or web logs started out as a place for people to keep journals, share ideas, and rant. They still do that, but now companies also use them to keep customers informed, and many savvy online entrepreneurs use blogs to make money using affiliate programs and advertising. Blogs are fast and easy to set up, especially with free blog services such as Blogger and Wordpress. Further, search engines love blogs, making them a great way to get traffic.

In Chapter 12, you learned about using eBay, Amazon.com, and storefronts. All of them offer a great way to get your products online quickly and, in the case of eBay and Amazon.com, affordably.

When working online, any of the above methods can work for you. Further, there is no rule that says you can only have one online presence. In fact, many website owners also have blogs and market their products through eBay. However, in this chapter I'm going to focus on building websites, as they still offer one of the best ways to make money online.

The Mistress of Your Own Domain

Before you can build your website, you need to create and buy a domain name. A domain name is the address or URL (universal resource locator) of your website. For example, WorkatHome-Success.com is the domain name for my website Work-at-Home Success. Choosing a domain should take you some time. Brainstorm many ideas, not only to get the best ones, but to have backups if the one you want is taken. Your list should include variations of your business name and topic keywords. Using the gardening idea, possible domain names are NancysOrganicGardening.com or TheGardeningBox.com (at this time, both these domain names are available for purchase).

When choosing a domain:

- Make it easy to remember.
- Keep it as short as possible.
- Use keywords related to your product or service.
- Start with letters at the beginning of the alphabet or a number. Directories like to alphabetize things. However, if by doing this your domain name violates rule #1 or #2, you may be better off skipping it. It's easier to remember workathomesuccess.com than aworkathomesuccess.com or 1workathomesuccess.com.
- Avoid using hyphens if you can. People forget to include hyphens when typing in your URL and it can be hard to tell someone your URL if you have to stop and mention the hyphens. "Wwwdotmyhyphendomainhyphen businessdotcom."
- Try to buy a .com if you can. People may remember your domain, but forget if its .net or .TV. Instead, they type in .com and end up at your competitor's site.
- Target your customers, but allow for expansion. If you sell designer jeans and your target is teenage girls, you can have a domain TeenJean.com. But if you want to expand your market to boys or women TeenJean.com doesn't fit. In that case, FemJeans.com or TotalJean.com might be better.

Buying a Domain

Some web hosts (see page 193 for hosting information) will include the purchase of your domain name if you buy hosting or you can purchase it through a domain registrar. I'm partial to Godaddy.com, at which I have over thirty domains registered. Godaddy.com is affordable at $8.99 per year, and sometimes less if you buy a domain with an alternate extension (e.g., .info). But there are other options. You can do a search in your favorite search engine for "domain registrars" to find a list of other registrars.

At the registrar website, you'll find a space to check the availability of your domain. If it's taken, try one of your other choices. Godaddy.com has a feature in which it can suggest ideas as well.

When you find a name that is available, follow the directions on the site for purchasing it. Some questions you'll be asked during the purchase will include:

- Do you want private registration? In this case, your contact information is not disclosed to people who might search WHO IS to find out who owns the domain name.
- How many years do you want to own the domain? Often the price goes down for each additional year you buy.
- Where do you want the domain to direct to? Or it may ask about server information. At this point, you want to choose the option to "park" your domain at the registrar. When you buy hosting, your hosting company will give you server information to input at the domain registrar. This will tell the registrar to send people to your host when your domain is accessed. Another option is domain forwarding. If you have an affiliate URL, a member website with your direct-sales company, or are using a free hosted blog (e.g., Blogger), you can buy a domain and have the registrar forward it to any URL you want.
- You may be offered special deals during the buying process. You can ignore these unless you're still looking for a web host. These may not be the best deals, but they may offer templates and hosting designed for the new web entrepreneur who's still learning the ropes. You can always move your website to a new host if you want.
- Don't forget to read all agreements and terms of service.

Hosting Your Website

Before your website can go live, it needs a place to exist on the web. Web hosts supply this space. Web-hosting services vary so you need to know what you want your website to do and then pick a web host that can provide the service to support your website.

Hosting features to consider are:

Storage: Unless you're running a few pages selling a specific item, you want to get as much storage as you can afford. This will allow you to add more features as you grow.

Bandwidth: The more bandwidth your host can provide, the more visitors your site can host simultaneously without crashing.

Transfer allowance: Each time someone accesses your website, data is delivered or transferred to them. web hosts provide a set amount of data transfers per month. If you exceed it, you may be charged extra.

E-mail: Most hosts offer online e-mail access (web mail) and POP3 e-mail accounts.

FrontPage extensions: If you're using Microsoft FrontPage to build your website and are using the scripting features the software includes, choose a web host that provides FrontPage extensions.

Web stats: Web stats will tell you how many people are visiting your site, what pages they're viewing, and much more.

CGI-Bin: FormMail and other scripts use cgi programming, for which you need a CGI-Bin folder.

PHP support: This scripting language can add features such as a message board to your site.

Server Side Includes: This is a scripting language that allows files to use information from other files. It's used with many scripts.

SQL or database: This is used for many features such as a discussion board or blog.

E-commerce: Handles shopping carts and payment processing.

Uptime percent: Web servers crash, so none will have 100 percent uptime. But you want an uptime that is close to 100 percent because when the server is down, so is your website.

Control panel: Through a control panel you can access your statistics, upload web pages, create e-mail accounts, activate FrontPage extensions or SQL database, and add other features.

Upgrades for growth: Many hosts have a series of features you may not think you need now, but will want to use in the future. Can you add a database if you need to? Can you upgrade to a bigger plan as your business grows?

Plug-ins: If you are not tech savvy, plug-in features are a great way to easily add features such as discussion boards, blogs, FAQ pages, and more to your website.

Tech support availability and methods: If you plan to make money with your website, don't settle for anything less than 24/7 phone tech support. There will be a time, usually in the middle of the night, that you discover your website isn't working. If it's not working, you aren't making money. At these times, you need help and fast, even if it's 2 A.M. Other technical support features include live chat, e-mail support, knowledge base of information, and discussion group.

Operating system: Just like Mac and PC use different systems to run, so do servers. Windows servers are great for people needing Microsoft-specific scripts such as Active Server Pages (ASP). Unix/Linux can run almost any other type of script and is usually a better choice if you'll be using any Perl or PHP scripting. Some web hosts offer both options. If you have questions, contact the host's customer or sales support and it can help you decide which option is best for your purpose.

FTP: Unless you're going to use a template offered by your host, you'll need a way to get your website from your computer (or your website designer's computer) to your host server and on the World Wide Web. Some web hosts have a system through the control panel through which you can find the file on your computer and upload it to your server. I find it easier to use an FTP (File Transfer Protocol) program from my local computer. You can find FTP software at *www.ipswitch.com/products/ws_ftp* or search for "ftp software" on your favorite browser.

Domain allowance: More and more web hosts are allowing clients to host multiple domains (websites) for the price of one. This can be a great option if you plan to build several websites. But again, check that all the features you need for the website you're building now are available.

Cost: What do you get for your money? As I mentioned, some sites will host your website for pennies, while others cost several hundred dollars a year. Cheaper isn't always better, so focus on the features you need to run your site and find the host that will provide the most options, the most reliably, at the best cost.

Free Versus Paid Hosting

Many people tell me they have no money to start a business and want to use a free hosting service. If you are really serious about making money on the Internet, you *must* pay for website hosting. Free hosting is great for posting family travels or fan fiction, but it's unprofessional for running a business, even if you use domain forwarding to mask the free website's long URL.

Free websites not only are unprofessional, but they affect the amount of money you earn because free isn't really free. In exchange for hosting your website, the free host will run ads on your Web pages. These aren't benign ads. They are pop ups, pop unders, and flashing banners, all of which are distracting and annoying to your visitors. Even if you have to go with a low-cost host, scrape the money together. I host my small websites with one host for $48 a year.

Choosing a Host

Now comes the hard part. If you do an Internet search for web hosting, you'll find more options than you can imagine. Once you access a hosting service, you're faced with more options. The basic package or the business package? Gold, platinum, or silver plans?

My recommendation is to network with web-mistresses you know or read reviews of hosting services. One place to check is CNET *http://reviews.cnet.com/web-hosting*. To choose a host, use the Website Checklist to compare plans.

Website Checklist

Features	Host Service Name	Host Service URL
Storage (MB)		
Bandwidth		
Transfer allowance (GB)		
Pop 3 e-mail accounts (how many?):		
Web-based:		
FrontPage extensions:		
Web statistics:		
CGI-Bin for scripts:		
PHP:		
Server Side Includes		
SQL:		
Uptime percent:		

Control panel:		
Upgrades for growth:		
Plug-ins:		
Tech support availability and methods:		
Operating system:		
FTP:		
Domain allowance		
Cost		

Building a Money-Making Website

Whether you're going to build your website yourself or hire someone to do it, you need to plot your vision, including purpose, content, and tone. Start by answering the following questions:

1. What is the purpose of the site? What do you want people to do when they visit the site? Learn and use resources listed? Buy something? A little of both?

2. How will the site make money? Are you selling your own creations? Using affiliate programs? Working with a wholesale drop shipper?

3. How will the income streams be integrated into the site? Will you have a single sales letter/page? Will you have ads?

4. If you're building a content site or selling multiple products, how can the information be categorized?

5. How will orders be processed? Will you need a shopping cart with full payment features? A third-party service such as Clickbank.com or PayPal?

6. Will you have a newsletter?

7. Will you have interactive features such as a message board?

8. Will you be using audio or video as part of the sale process?

9. How will customers be able to get in touch with you?

10. What is the tone of the site? Will it be professional or whimsical? Will the graphics be photos or clipart?

Building a Website

While it can be helpful to learn HTML and other website coding languages, you don't have to know anything about programming to build a website. Instead you can:

Use a template from your host provider: Many website hosts offer templates and online website-building support. Simply choose a template, add text, upload a picture and you've got a website. Many even have plug-and-play add-ons that you can use, such as message boards and blogs. As convenient as these are, they usually aren't as visually appealing and don't have the versatility that building a site from scratch offers.

Use website-building software: FrontPage (now Expressions) and Dreamweaver are examples of robust website-building software. Using software gives you more flexibility and options than the web-host templates do. Further, you have complete control over the layout. However, some programs include unneeded coding. Further, to make maximum use of the programs, it helps to know some coding. Finally, the most powerful website-building programs such as Dreamweaver can cost several hundred dollars. I'm using free software called KompoZer (*http://kompozer.sourceforge.net*) that is fairly easy to use, but doesn't come with premade templates.

Hire a designer: If you have a vision of how you want your site to look but don't know HTML from HTTP, you can hire a designer to build your website. Design firms have several people working on a project and they can help you flesh out ideas to make your site better. However, they can be expensive. A freelance web designer can have as much if not more experience and cost less to hire than a design firm. But she may not be as reliable with timelines.

Finding a designer involves research and getting recommendations. If you see websites that you like, check the bottom of the page to see if the designer is listed or contact the owner to find out who the designer is.

If you want to hire a freelancer, you can use one of the freelance sites such as eLance.com to post your project and get bids. I particularly like Rentacoder.com for web-design work that involves scripts or special coding. These resources offer an extra bit of financial protection by holding your money in escrow until you deem the project finished to your satisfaction.

Use the checklist below to help you choose the best designer for your project.

Web Design Checklist

1. How is the work billed? Hourly fee? Flat rate?

2. If you'll be billed an hourly rate, how much time will the project take? Will you be notified in advance if the time is exceeding the quote?

3. What is included in the price quote? Number of pages? Special coding?

4. Will you be sent proofs throughout the process?

5. Does the company provide maintenance and updates? What are the fees?

6. What other sites has it built?

7. What is the feedback from previous clients?

8. How will the project be delivered? (Uploaded for you? Delivered on CD?)

Before hiring a designer, have the concept for your site completely mapped out. Designers can't read your mind, so you need a clear vision of what you want on the site, how it should look and feel, and what functions it needs to have. If you have samples of graphics you want to use, send them to the designer. Have your content (text) prepared and ready to put on the page.

Many designers want at least part of their fee upfront. *Never* send money without a written agreement that spells out the details of your project. Make sure that the contract specifies that the work is work-for-hire (contract) and that all aspects of the project (pictures, text, etc.) are owned by you (you hold the copyright). Ask for a copy of the work on CD to have in case your server crashes or your web designer's computer crashes.

Copyright Issues with Graphics

Just because something is online, doesn't mean it's free to use. Many graphics and scripts have copyrights attached to them and using them without permission can land you in a heap of trouble.

What Goes on a Web Page

Regardless of what method you use to create an online presence, your web page needs to have the "four Cs": Content, Credibility, Contact, and Customers.

Content

There is a saying, "Content is king." And it's true. Content is where the money is. To have money-making content on your site, your content needs to:

- Fit your product and the market you're targeting.
- Fulfill customers' expectations.
- Be well written and organized.
- Be interesting.
- Be updated regularly.
- Match your keywords.

Credibility

When I first posted WorkAtHomeSuccess.com online in 1998, there were only a handful of other work-at-home websites. By 2000 there were hundreds of them. The problem was that many of them were run by people who had no experience in working at home. Many of these websites promoted assembly work or mailing programs. When their visitors got hurt from the scams, the websites owners' credibility as a reliable source of work-at-home information was shot. The Internet is everywhere, and it never forgets. One bad move, and it's all over. That's how important your credibility is.

To create credibility, your website needs to answer:

■ Why should customers believe you? What is your experience or knowledge of the topic?

■ Why should they believe your information? What is it about your offer that is more credible than what others offer?

■ What have you done to expand your credibility? You don't get credibility once and it's done. You must always be learning and building your knowledge and experience. Reading, networking, researching, and keeping abreast of new developments and trends in your topic will maintain and grow your expertise and credibility.

Contact

If content is king, your list of contacts is gold. Many people will visit a website, but aren't ready to buy. However, they may be willing to give you their name and e-mail in exchange for free information such as a newsletter, free report, or e-course. In fact, most people will not buy on the first visit to your site, so creating a database of potential prospects is the only way you'll eventually sell to them. By gathering names and e-mail addresses you can continuously build relationships, credibility, and sell to the members of the list.

Customers (Traffic)

Without customers, you have nothing but a nice website. To help your website attract traffic, include the following on your web pages (including blogs, eBay, etc.):

- Topic keywords in the meta tags (see the website-building section in this chapter for an explanation of meta tags.)
- Topic keywords in the content
- Content that grabs the visitor's attention as soon as the page loads (see the information on copywriting in the marketing chapter)

The Money Is in the Keywords

You've run across the term "keywords" a lot already in this book. A keyword is a term or phrase that identifies the ideas and concepts presented on your website. Keywords are important because search engines use them to index and list your website. Many advertising services such as Google's AdWords use keywords to determine what ads are fed onto other websites through its AdSense program.

Develop a list of keywords using Google's Keyword Tool or Good Keywords software (*www.goodkeywords.com*), both of which are free. To get more details and statistics on keywords, you can use the paid service at Wordtracker.com (*www.wordtracker.com/index.html*). Another resource that is less expensive than Wordtracker is Ad Word Analyzer (*www.adwordanalyzer.com*).

LAWS OF WORK-AT-HOME SUCCESS #㉑
Understanding and using keywords correctly is crucial to online success!

While much of what ends up on your website depends on your site's topic, there are some features that should always be included.

Your logo: Your designer (if you hire one) can help you create this or you can use a graphic or logo software to help you. Your logo should be catchy yet fit with the theme and mood of your site.

Tagline: This is a phrase that sums up what your website is about. You don't necessarily have to have one, but it can be a great way to help customers remember you. At WorkAtHomeSuccess .com it's "Balance Work and Family . . . Work at Home!"

Privacy statement: Let people know what you'll be doing or not doing with any information you gather from them. Some websites will sell your name, e-mail, and other information you give them. If you don't intend to do that, let your visitors know so they can feel good about giving you their information.

Contact information: Make it easy for visitors to get in touch with you. I recommend using a contact form as opposed to giving your e-mail. This will help prevent farming of your e-mail (gathering your e-mail address to spam you).

About Us page: Let your visitors know about you and your business.

E-mail capture (newsletter, giveaway, etc.): Use a form to offer a newsletter or free giveaway in exchange for your visitors' names and e-mails. The big money in online businesses comes from building an opt-in e-mail list. This is covered in greater detail in the online marketing chapter.

FAQ page: As your site grows, you'll find that you get the same questions over and over again. One way to manage this is to have a page that answers these Frequently Asked Questions (FAQ).

Other features to consider include:

Discussion boards: Forums allow people to interact with you and other visitors, thereby creating a sense of community.

Blogs: You should have a blog for reasons that will be discussed in the marketing section. You can sign up for a hosted blog through Blogger.com or Wordpress.com and link to it from your website. Or you can download a blog script and host it on your own servers alongside your website. Either way, get one and post something related to your site topic three or four times a week.

Free stuff: I love free stuff. You probably love free stuff. Everyone loves free stuff. You can offer free reports, newsletters, articles, even software on your website.

Members-Only site: Some sites make their money through memberships while others offer free membership. If you have a member site, make sure that the materials are worth the price of admission. You'll need a script to help manage access (registration, usernames, passwords, etc.), but you can find them free or for reasonable cost online or through your web host.

Live chat: Live chat allows people on your website to get in contact with you in real time to ask questions or get help with your product or service. While you can get free chat-room scripts or services, live-help chat services usually have a fee with it.

Podcasting: Online recordings provide a great way to keep your customers informed of current trends in your industry or to teach them the best ways to use your products and services. They can listen right from your website or they can download your audio onto their MP3 to listen to while they are on the run.

The Look and Feel of the Site

On the web, less is almost always more. Study websites and make notes on features that you like or don't like. Evaluate the layout, color scheme, and format of the Web page. Read the content and evaluate its relevance, quality, and presentation.

Ideally websites should have:

- *Lots of white space*—cluttered sites are distracting and unappealing.
- *Content that is organized, concise, and relevant.*
- *Readable font and color scheme.* The main parts of the page should have white space with black font, except for hyperlinks, which should be blue.
- *Consistent and easy navigation.* Most sites have navigational links or buttons along the top or left-hand side of the page to help visitors find the information they need. If a page is long, using "Top" or "Bottom" links within the page helps your visitors get to the information they want on the page. Have a "Home" option so visitors can get back to where they started and include a "Site Map" in your navigation to help people find what they need faster.
- *Browser compatibility.* When I redesigned my site, many Firefox users had trouble viewing it. Check that your site appears correctly in the major browsers used by web surfers such as Explorer and Firefox.
- *Keywords and meta tags.* This is vitally important particularly if you hope to have search-engine ranking. Search engines index sites based on the hidden codes that describe your site as well as the use of the keywords within your site.
- *Quick-loading pages.* Don't be overly generous with flash and graphics, as they will slow your website down. If the visitor is like me, they might not wait around for your site to load.

Websites *don't* need:

- *Frames.* Some browsers don't support frames, so it's best to avoid them.
- *Pop-ups.* Most people block these anyway, but if they don't, they'll be annoyed by them.
- *Flash* (unless you are selling flash-related services). Flash is fun for entertainment sites or for presentations that visitors indicate they want to view. But you don't want the entry into your website to be flash. Remember, people are visiting your site for information. Making them sit through the loading of a flash presentation slows them down.
- *Odd noises, automatic audio or music.* Many people are either startled or annoyed by noise. Like flash, it's better to give your visitors the option of hearing music or your pitch.
- *Lots of banners, buttons, and other graphics.* Too many banners and buttons, especially those that have animation, create sensory overload and distract from the content of your site.

Website-Building Checklist

Below is a list to help keep track of items and features to include on your website.

- Home page (index.html)
- About Us page
- Privacy and Disclosures page
- Contact page
- Site map
- FAQ
- Content pages
- Order page
- Checkout and payment page

- Thank you page for order
- Thank you page for subscribing to newsletter
- Meta tags and keywords on each page

Plan for Work-at-Home Success

1. Learn about and understand the importance of keywords.

2. Do keyword searches in your topic areas.

3. Decide what type of online presence you want, such as website, blog, or storefront.

4. Research hosting and domain names.

5. Develop the four Cs—Content, Credibility, Contact, and Customers—for your site.

6.   Create your website yourself or hire a designer.

Part Four

THE BUSINESS
OF RUNNING
A BUSINESS

CHAPTER SIXTEEN

Making It Legal

WOULDN'T IT BE GREAT IF YOU COULD COME UP WITH AN IDEA, hang a shingle (or post a website), and be in business? As easy as that would make business start-up, there are a host of legalities you need to address before taking that first customer.

Legal Structure

The legal form of your business will depend on several factors such as the number of owners, liability, and tax situation.

Sole Proprietor

Many people who start a one-man show begin as a *sole proprietor*. The advantage of a sole proprietorship is that it's easy to set up. You don't have any complicated paperwork, and it doesn't require any special business identification numbers when filing your taxes. The downside to a sole proprietorship is that you are the business, which means all the liability is on you. Creditors or people filing suit can come after your home and personal assets.

Partnerships

If you're going into to business with a buddy, you'll need to form a *partnership*. The advantages of a partnership include the ability to pool money and resources from all members of the partnership, and sharing liability as well. The disadvantage of a partnership is that control is shared among the partners. One way around this is through a *limited partnership*, in which partners share in financing the business and taking some liability, but have little control over the operations of the business. Whether you choose a general or limited partnership, extensive paperwork is needed to create the partnership agreement, and you may be required to register your partnership in your state. A lawyer will be able to give you more details on the requirements for setting up a partnership in your state.

Corporation

Imagine having the letters "Inc." after your business name. When you form a corporation, you create an entity that exists separate from you. Corporations come in a variety of shapes and sizes depending on the number of people, business purpose, and tax situation. The advantages of incorporating include liability resting solely on the business so your personal assets aren't at risk, possible tax benefits, and the ability to raise money through stock. The disadvantages of corporations include the high cost of getting it set up and extensive paperwork. One option is incorporating as a Limited Liability Corporation (LLC). It has many of the characteristics of a partnership and corporation; however, it can be set up by a single person. It still has some expense and paperwork hassle, but it's less extensive than creating a General or S Corp. The benefits of an LLC include the tax advantages of a partnership and the liability protection of a corporation. Consult a lawyer to help you navigate all your business structure options.

Permits, Licenses, and Sales Tax

I don't have a business license. I don't need one because my county doesn't require it. But I don't think that's the norm. In the other two places that I started a business, I was required to get a permit. To determine if your locality requires one, contact your local government business office. You can find its number under the city or county name in your phone book.

Even if your local government doesn't require a business license, you still may need a license or permit to operate your business. Many states have policies and registration requirements for specific business fields such as animal or child care, catering or food services, counseling, grooming and spa, and law. If your local government doesn't know if you need a specialty permit, you can use the Internet to research the industry guidelines in your state.

Sales Tax Permits

If you're selling a tangible item, that is something that you can hold, you may need to get a sales tax permit, which allows you to collect sales tax and pay it to the state. Your local government business office should be able to help you or you can contact your state's sales tax office directly.

If you'll be running an online business, ask your state's sales tax person about whether or not you need to collect tax just on customers who reside in your state or everyone. While there have been efforts to manage this on a national level through the Streamlined Sales and Use Tax Agreement, nothing has been made into policy as of yet.

What's in a Name?

Naming your business may be the most important creative decision you make. It will become a part of your business brand and marketing effort. I find that creating a list of words describing your business and the image you want to portray, and then experimenting with different word combos is the best way to develop business name ideas. Some things to consider are:

- *Simplicity:* Your business name should be simple and straightforward. This is especially true if you plan to take your business online and have a domain name that is the same as your business name.

- *Easy to remember:* Have you ever seen a name, title, or business that you wanted to look up in the phone book or online, only to later forget what it's called? I have, but then again, I'm getting old.

- *Describes your business:* Make it easy for your clients or customers to choose you by having your business name include a description of your business.

- *Allow flexibility to add services:* In the previous point, I suggested that your business name include something about what you do, but don't make it so specific that you can't expand your service, product line, or market. Instead of "Jane's Copywriting" choose "Jane's Writing Services" or "Jane's PR and Design."

- *Check that the domain name is available.* At Godaddy. com, you can search for domains. If the domain you want isn't available it can suggest alternatives, making it a great resource for brainstorming business names.

- *If you are going to run your business online or outside your local area, research trademarks (www.uspto.gov)* and copyrights *(www.copyright.gov)* to make sure your business name won't infringe on someone's intellectual property rights.

Fictitious Name Statement

If you've chosen a business name that's something other than your given name or your corporation's name, it's likely you'll need to submit a fictitious name statement to your local government office that regulates business. For example, if your name is Jane Smith, but your business will be called Acme Coaching Services, you need to file a Doing Business As form with your local city or county government business office, and have the information about your business printed in the newspaper. Corporations don't need to file a fictitious name statement unless it will do business under another name. For example, if your business is Acme Corporation but you'll be using Acme Coaching Services, then you need to file a fictitious name statement.

The information collected and printed in the newspaper includes your business name, the owner(s) name(s), location of the business, and the nature of the business. In some localities, you can submit the form and proper fee, and the government agency will file it and list it in the paper. In other localities you may need to contact the newspaper yourself. Your local government department that regulates businesses can let you know about this.

Zoning

Many areas have restrictions on home business that you'll want to check out before your nosy neighbor turns you in for a zoning violation. Zoning laws related to business were created to help preserve neighborhoods' aesthetic charm. No one wants a neighbor hanging a gaudy sign on the house or operating a toxic waste dump in the backyard. Because many people can run a home business that won't increase traffic, require signs, or use dangerous materials, many communities have waivers that will allow you to work from home. Check with the city or county business office about zoning issues and waivers if necessary.

Aside from city or county zoning, also check to see if your homeowners' association, or lease if you rent, has any restrictions on a home-based business. Again, if you don't plan to increase traffic by seeing customers in your home, putting up a sign, or using dangerous materials, you usually can get permission.

Intellectual Property Protection

I just finished reading a news item in which a romance novelist with over 100 books to her credit has been accused of plagiarism. In fact, in the news report I read, she actually admitted to lifting information from nonfiction resources to use in her books, claiming she didn't know she had to cite her sources. It may not seem like such a big deal to use a phrase or picture found in a book or online, that is until it's your phrase or picture being used without your permission. There are several intellectual-property protection services you should use to protect your rights.

Trademark

A trademark is a symbol or word associated with a product, service, or company. Most have the letters R or TM next to them. Before committing to your business or domain name, it's a good idea to do a trademark search to ensure that you don't infringe on another company's trademark. At the same time, you should consider trademarking your business name, logo, and even your slogan to prevent other people from using it. You can use the trademark symbols on your materials without registering, but to protect yourself fully, you need to register for a trademark. To learn more about trademarks, visit the U.S. Patent and Trademark Office online at *www.uspto.gov.*

Copyrights

Several years ago, I came across a website that had copied, verbatim, several pages of my website including the "About Me" page. I contacted the owner letting her know that she was in violation of copyright laws. While she did remove the material, she wrote back telling me that ideas can't be copyrighted. She's right. However, she didn't take my ideas; she took my words verbatim, including my life story, and passed it off as hers. That's copyright infringement. Copyrights cover original works such as literary, dramatic, artistic, and other published and unpublished works. Copyrighted work cannot be used by anyone other than the author without permission. You can copyright your website and other written or artistic works simply by adding "Copyright" or the copyright symbol ©. But if you want to sue someone for stealing your work, you'll need to register for a copyright at *www.copyright.gov*.

Patents

A patent provides rights of an invention to its inventor for twenty years. The idea is to protect the inventor and ensure she gets full financial benefits before someone else can use the idea. If you have an idea for the next best gizmo, don't wait, find a good patent attorney. Short of that, you can check out Tamara Monosoff's book, *The Mom Inventors Handbook* or *The Carey Formula: Your Ideas Are Worth Millions* by Barbara Carey for insights into the process of developing an idea to patent, produce, and market.

LAWS OF WORK-AT-HOME SUCCESS #㉒
Don't take your first customer until you have secured all appropriate licenses, permits, and protections.

Plan for Work-at-Home Success

1. Determine your legal structure. Contact a lawyer for advice on the best structure for your business idea.

2. Contact your local government office for information on permits, licensing, zoning, and fictitious name statements.

3. Make a list of potential business names and ask for feedback from a mentor or friend.

4. Make sure your business name and materials don't infringe on anyone's intellectual property rights. Take steps to protect your rights by registering for the appropriate rights protection.

CHAPTER SEVENTEEN
Money Matters

YOU'VE PICKED UP THIS BOOK BECAUSE YOU WANT TO MAKE MONEY from home. At the root of it, this book is all about money. But as we learned in Chapter 3, money matters are not always pleasant. Accounting, budgets, taxes . . . my eyes are droopy just thinking about it. However, money, not just the money you make but the money you invest and how well you manage it all, will play a key role in your success.

Finding Start-Up Money

While it's not impossible to start a business without any capital outlay, the reality is that there are expenses involved in running a business. But you don't need to max out your credit cards to start your business. The following ideas suggest many ways to find or create extra cash to fund your business.

Save up. Each week or month, put a portion of your earnings into a special savings account just for your business start-up.

Have a yard sale. Everyone has unwanted and unused stuff taking up space in their homes. Have a yard sale or sell it on eBay and use the proceeds to fund your business.

Ask a family member for a loan. Be careful when you take money from family. Have clear terms on whether it's a loan or a gift. Further, be prepared to deal with questions and even ridicule from your "angel" investor.

Tap into savings. Most people are already woefully underfunding their savings, so only use your savings if you're 110 percent committed to success and repaying your savings account.

Use credit cards. This is another area in which most people need to be careful. Make a plan to pay your debt as quickly as possible.

Apply for credit from vendors. Do you need materials or products to run your business? You may be able to start a credit line with vendors and pay them back as your inventory sells. This is like any other credit line and in fact may have higher interest rates, so enter into this type of situation carefully.

Investigate seller financing. If you're buying a franchise or an existing business, you may be able to get credit or financing from the company. Read all the terms and be sure that you can make the payments.

Apply for home equity lines and assets. Like your savings account, you don't want to use your home equity or other assets unless you're committed to your business' success or can sell your business assets to repay your savings.

Go to the bank. Many banks have loan programs for business start-up. Create a professional business plan that not only outlines your product or service, but also how you'll get clients and your money projections.

Apply for government grants and loans. Federal, state, and local governments have loan and grant programs to help small business. You can learn more about government programs by visiting your local Small Business Administration or SCORE office or visit them online at *www.sba.gov* and *www.score.org*.

Apply for professional association loans. Many associations have loans or grants to help you start a business. Search online for associations and groups in your industry to learn more.

Borrow from retirement. If you take an early withdrawal from your retirement savings, you'll probably have to pay taxes and penalties. Plus, you'll have less money for retirement. There is a 401(k) called the Solo 401(k) plan that allows you to make withdrawals for business or hardship if needed. Rollovers from other 401(k)s are allowed. There are some restrictions, such as they are designed for solo entrepreneurs, not partnerships. Your financial planner can better provide the details you need regarding Solo 401(k)s.

Look into venture capital. Venture capital firms invest their members' money in high-risk start-up companies that have the possibility of creating big returns. Getting venture capital requires a top-notch business plan that shows potential for above-average returns. To learn more about venture capital and find databases of firms, visit *www.vfinance.com*.

Find an angel investor. Somewhere between asking your friends and family for money and applying for venture capital is the angel investor. Angel investors are usually wealthy individuals who invest in start-up businesses. Like venture capitalists, an angel investor gets a share of the business pie or collateral in exchange for his or her investment. Networking is your best bet for finding an angel investor.

Counting Your Cash

Making money is great. I love going online to see my affiliate commissions and other sales income. But keeping track of money isn't just about what's coming in, it's also about tracking what's going out. If you don't like budgeting, you may not like business financial management much either, but it's crucial to keeping your business in the black. To organize your money matters:

- *Keep all business-related bills and receipts.*
- *Print out receipts for online sales. Don't leave these in your e-mail box.* If your computer crashes, you won't have proof of your purchase to verify a tax deduction.
- *Open a separate business account.* The IRS prefers that you keep your business money separate from your personal money.
- *Know your overhead and running costs.* A $10 service here and a $40 service there can add up. Make a list of your regular operating expenses so you know how much it costs you to do business.
- *Keep track of what you're owed.* Not everyone pays on time, so keep a folder of the unpaid invoices or use money management software to keep track of who's paid you and who hasn't.

LAWS OF WORK-AT-HOME SUCCESS #㉓
The better you organize and manage your money, the more you save and make!

Accounts Receivable

So far you know how to find start-up capital and how to manage the money going out. Now you need a system for tracking the money that's coming in. This is important because there will be times when you don't get money that's owed to you. I have had affiliate merchants fail to pay commissions and contract employers fail to pay for work I'd done. On several occasions money that was owed to me came late, and after a lot of hassle with the check writer. To keep your business operating in the black, develop a system to track the money you're owed.

- *Create a system to track your accounts.* With affiliate marketing, keep a list or spreadsheet on the companies you promote and when they pay. Make it a point to check your affiliate statistics and log it in your spreadsheet each month.
- *If you're providing a product or service, use invoices not just to bill, but to track who owes you what.* Business finance software can help you with generating invoices and accounts receivable reports.
- *Send invoices in a timely manner and give a due date for payment.*
- *Include a late payment penalty such as 4 percent interest to encourage timely payment.*
- *Check the payment against the invoice* to make sure the customer paid what he was billed.

Not Getting Paid?

At some point, you may be in a situation in which someone doesn't pay you. To collect the money you're owed:

- *Use contracts in your business dealings* to give you leverage when someone fails to pay.

■ *Have a system for dealing with customer dissatisfaction,* as some people don't pay when they're not happy with your product or service.

■ *If you have not received payment, send a second notice as a reminder.* Bills do get lost and misplaced.

■ *If you still aren't paid, ask to speak to the person in charge of writing the check to find out what's going on.*

■ *Send a certified letter with a return receipt reminding the client of the amount due and a due date.* This shows you're serious about collecting the money and now have proof if you end up going to small claims court.

■ *Never threaten, embarrass, or expose the client.* It is tempting to do so, especially if you're doing business with a large company. But there are rules to debt collection, one of them being that you can't harass or threaten.

■ *If the bill is big enough and justifies the money and effort, you can go to small claims court to collect the debt.* If not, it might be better to take the nonpayment as a loss on your taxes.

■ *Don't continue working with deadbeats* without getting payment upfront.

Pay Yourself

There isn't a financial planner or guru who doesn't tell you to pay yourself first. And you should. But you need to pay your business expenses and reinvest in your business as well. The formula I use to pay myself and invest in my business is:

1. Invest 10 percent of my gross profit into savings.
2. Pay all business-related expenses.
3. Set aside 15 to 20 percent for taxes.
4. Invest 15 to 30 percent back into the business.
5. Use the remainder, when needed, to live on.

Other business owners establish a salary they pay themselves regularly. If your business is a LLC or other legal entity, you'll need to develop a salary, as taking money from the pot whenever you want it can be illegal.

Lowering Business Expenses

Business expenses can rack up pretty quickly. However, the less you spend on your business, the more you get to keep. There are a few key ways to keep control of your business spending. Be sure to use free resources. You can find a host of free resources and information online that can help you with your business. You can use programs like Mail Washer to screen e-mails, KompoZer to build websites, and FormMail to manage online forms. All of these are free. Take advantage of sales and rebates. Whenever you can, buy used. If you have to invest money, consider buying a used or refurbished item. Learn how to barter. There are many entrepreneurs just like you who are willing to trade services. All you have to do is ask.

Taxes

Some people tell me they don't want to work for themselves because they have to pay taxes. I hate to break it to you, but if you work, whether it's for yourself or someone else, you have to pay taxes. While doing your taxes is a bit more involved when you work for yourself, the cost savings and benefits are well worth the effort. And it's not that hard once you learn the ropes (or hire someone to do it for you). The first step is to keep track of all your expenses.

Indirect expenses are expenses that are not directly related to your business, but are still incurred. You can deduct a portion usually based on the percentage of the expense that relates to your business. These include:

- Mortgage or rent
- Utilities (electric, etc.)
- Security system
- Homeowners' association fees

Direct expenses are those directly related to doing business, including:

- *Phone services.* You can't deduct the cost of your main phone line, but you can deduct long-distance calls, voice mail, three-way calling, and other features related to your business. You can deduct the cost of an additional phone line for business use.
- *Internet access.* If you also use the Internet for fun, it becomes an indirect expense and you need to determine the percentage of time your Internet access is used for business.
- Postage
- Auto expenses
- Business travel, including meals and entertainment
- Office equipment and supplies
- Office furniture
- Professional services
- Professional education
- Association dues
- Memberships and subscriptions
- Health insurance
- Retirement plans

While you're allowed many deductions, you don't want to take advantage of the IRS's generosity by deducting nonbusiness-related items, as there are penalties for doing so. Because there are rules and restrictions, it is recommended that you consult with a tax professional. At the very least, get a copy of the IRS Publication 587: Business Use of Your Home (*www.irs.gov/ publications/p587/index.html*).

Estimated Tax Payments

The IRS has a pay-as-you-go tax system. If you're currently employed, you pay your taxes monthly. Fortunately, self-employed people only have to pay quarterly in April, June, September, and January. More good news is that you can estimate your deductions when calculating your payments (something your boss can't do for you). The only thing to be careful of is that you pay enough to cover the tax bill. While the IRS understands that it is estimated tax, it can penalize you if the tax owed on your yearly return due in April is over $1,000. Set aside money each time you get paid to be used to make your quarterly estimated payment. Keep track of your expenses. Use spreadsheet or money management software to calculate your monthly and quarterly expenses. After you have worked for yourself for one year, you can use what you owed the previous year and divide by four to estimate your tax payment.

Social Security Versus EIN

If you're operating as a sole proprietor, you can use your social security number as your tax ID. However, if you're in a partnership or other entity, you'll need to apply for an Employer Identification Number (EIN). You'll need to get an EIN if you have employees, withhold taxes on income, or have a Keogh plan. To learn more about EIN visit the IRS online at: *www.irs.gov/businesses/small/article/0,,id=97872,00.html*.

Remember to consult with a tax professional for help.

Insurance

Dealing with insurance is usually a hassle. However, it is extremely important to have the right coverage. While your homeowner or renter's insurance may cover some aspects of your home office, it probably won't cover everything. Plus, insurance isn't just about covering your property and equipment, it's also about protecting you from liability. If you have employees or use your car in the course of doing business, you'll need insurance for them as well. Don't take a chance on your financial future by not having adequate insurance. Contact your insurance agent to inquire about coverage for:

- Property damage to your home office
- Liability coverage if you see clients in your home
- Product liability coverage
- Loss of business
- Employer liability and workers comp if you hire employees
- Additional auto coverage if you use your auto in the course of doing business
- Health insurance
- Disability insurance

Plan for Work-at-Home Success

1. Start your business right by getting your finances in order before you begin your business.

2. Find start-up money.

3. Create a plan to reinvest some of your money back into your business as well as into a retirement account.

4. Organize your receipts and finances to ensure you take advantages of tax benefits.

5. Contact your insurance company to make sure you and your business have adequate coverage in the case of loss or lawsuit.

CHAPTER EIGHTEEN

It Takes a Village

YOU MAY BE IN BUSINESS FOR YOURSELF, but you shouldn't be by yourself. Even if you're a die-hard do-it-yourselfer, surrounding yourself with knowledgeable, experienced people will make running your business so much easier. If you don't believe me, go back and read the Success Profiles of the women in this book. All of them indicated they had and were grateful to mentors, coaches, and support professionals.

Mentors and Coaches

I haven't read a success-oriented book yet that doesn't recommend finding a mentor or coach. And it's a good idea. Why reinvent the wheel? Instead, find someone who has achieved the success you want and do what she does. Imagine what your real estate portfolio would be if you could follow Donald Trump around for a day (assuming you didn't get fired). But mentors and coaches can do much more than tell you how to do things.

They can offer feedback on new ideas. They're an excellent source for resources and networking. And they can keep you up when you're feeling down.

There are several ways to find mentors and coaches. The first step is to network with people in your industry either online or off. Get to know people and discover which ones you like and seem to have the success you're looking for. Offer to take them to lunch and see if they are receptive to helping you. Sometimes people are too busy or don't want to share their secrets. That's okay. Find someone else.

Another option is to get a job or apprentice with someone in your industry. The movie *The Pursuit of Happyness* tells the true story of Chris Gardner, a homeless single father who took an unpaid training course at Dean Witter, and within six years started his own firm. Learning from the source is a great way to get the basics from which you can launch your own business.

You can also hire a coach. Today there are coaches for everything from living happily to finding the best career. And there are business coaches who can help with developing your idea and creating profitable marketing plans. Coaches vary in price and usually will talk to you in person or by phone one to four times a month. Do extensive research on a coach before hiring her. Check references and learn about her specialties.

You can get a group of coaches and mentors by joining a mastermind group. I finally joined one for work-at-home moms a year ago and the impact on my life is amazing. Even though I had many years of work-at-home experience under my belt, I finally realized that two heads (or many heads) are better than one. Through a group, you'll have access to many brains from which to pick gems of information and resources. You can find partners, get feedback, and network to create even more opportunities.

Lawyers

Contract and tax materials are all written in English. I usually understand each individual word printed on them. But I have the darnedest time understanding what they say. Enter the lawyer, a master legalese translator. A lawyer can decipher contracts and tax documents and set up your business structure for maximum protection. Lawyers can assist you in protecting your business, such as registering for patents or trademarks. Further, they can advise you on employee and other business issues.

At the very least, you'll want to choose a lawyer who is knowledgeable about small business. However, depending on your business you may need more than one lawyer, each specializing in a specific area such as business structure, contracts, or intellectual property protection.

When choosing a lawyer, start by getting referrals from other business owners you know and trust. You can also check with your accountant or other business professionals you work with for their recommendations.

Accountant

If you don't know the difference between accrual versus cash basis accounting, and you don't want to figure it out, an accountant can help. An accountant can help you set up your bookkeeping system and assist with your taxes.

If you feel confident managing your finances or using good bookkeeping software, you may not need an accountant. But good money management is crucial to your success, so don't overlook the value an accountant can offer, particularly at tax time.

Vendors and Suppliers

Will you need raw materials to create your products? Will you be buying items in large quantities, whether it's CDs or paperclips? Vendors and suppliers provide you with the necessary goods or services to help you do your business. Because the quality of product and service you get from your vendors will affect the quality of product and service you supply to your customers, pick your vendors and suppliers carefully. Cheaper isn't always better, so don't just shop for price but for quality and customer service as well.

If the products you buy are used to create your product or service, you may be eligible to buy your supplies wholesale and avoid paying sales tax. You'll need to show the wholesaler a permit to receive this savings. Contact your local or state government for information on getting this permit.

Getting Help Without Hiring Employees

Starting your business, you'll do and be everything in your business: manufacturer, copywriter, accountant, saleswoman, web mistress, etc. But as your business grows, you'll come to a point where it's not feasible to do it all. Fortunately, you don't need to hire an administrative assistant and deal with the hassles of becoming an employer. Instead, you can hire freelancers who can work on a one-time project or assist you whenever you need the extra hands.

You can find freelance help for writing your business plan, creating your website, writing marketing materials, answering your e-mail, setting up appointments, and more. To make the most of freelance help, do your research and choose people who have proven experience as shown by their portfolios and references. Start by asking for references from your mentor or mastermind group. Elance (*www.elance.com*) and Guru.com (*www.guru.com*) are good resources to find help as well.

LAWS OF WORK-AT-HOME SUCCESS #24
Hiring help can free up your time to focus on those tasks that make money.

Plan for Work-at-Home Success

1. Find a business buddy, mastermind group, or mentor to share your ideas with and get feedback from on your business activities.

2. Get referrals for a good lawyer and accountant.

3. Research quality vendors and service providers. Find out if you can save by being a frequent customer or with a wholesale tax permit.

4. Determine which activities you don't like or take too much time, and hire freelancers to do those tasks.

CHAPTER NINETEEN

The Business Plan

WHILE SOME PEOPLE FALL INTO WORKING AT HOME BY ACCIDENT, eventually they develop some sort of plan to keep their business on track. Having a plan not only will help you succeed, it will help you succeed more quickly.

The best analogy for the importance of a business plan is that it's a road map. Imagine you wanted to drive from California to New York. You could jump in the car and head east; however, odds are you'd end up having to backtrack or drive further because you ended up in Minnesota or Virginia. With a road map, you can highlight your exact route and find alternative routes when needed. Instead of a week, you could get to New York in days. A business plan does the same thing. It highlights important areas of your business so you can focus on making money.

LAWS OF WORK-AT-HOME SUCCESS #㉕
If you fail to plan, you plan to fail.

There are four steps to putting together an effective business plan.

Step One: Research

Before you can write your plan, research and answer the following:

1. What is your business and how is it different from other businesses in the same industry?

2. What are your strengths, weaknesses, opportunities, and risks? (SWOT)

3. Who is your target market(s)?

4. Who is the competition and how do they differ from you and each other?

5. What are people willing to pay for what you're offering?

6. What will it cost you to do business?

7. How much can you make?

SWOT Analysis

A SWOT is an outline of your strengths, weaknesses, opportunities, and threats. A SWOT analysis will give you a quick overview of your business' status and areas you need to address in your business plan.

- Strengths—What are your strengths? What skills and knowledge do you have that makes you ideal for this business?
- Weaknesses—What are your weaknesses? What skills and knowledge do you need to learn to make your business a success?
- Opportunities—What opportunities exist that make this a good time for your business? For example, with societal acceptance of global warming, the green revolution can be seen as an opportunity.
- Threats—What threats are there to your success? Is there stiff competition? Is it difficult to get a permit or license for your specific business idea?

Step Two: What Will It Cost?

The next step in the business-plan process is to determine how much it is going to cost you to start and run your business.

1. Materials to create your product
2. Equipment to do business or provide your service
3. Hiring help or freelancers
4. One-time and ongoing services needed to conduct business
5. Permits, licenses, and other legal details
6. Marketing materials such as business cards
7. Running marketing campaigns
8. Postage, packaging, etc. for delivering your product or services
9. Travel
10. Other expenses related to your business

Step Three: How Much Money Will Your Business Make?

This is the challenging step because you really don't know how much you're going to make, until you're making it. Some tips to help include:

1. Set income goals.
2. Determine a price for your product or service. Research what others are charging. Also be willing to play with the price. Some people have found that they made more sales when they raised the price. Go figure.
3. Calculate how many sales you'd need to meet your goal income. For example, if you're selling books on Amazon.com and the average book is $6 and you want to earn $40,000, you'd need to sell approximately 128 books a week.

Step Four: Write the Business Plan

Now it's time to put all your research together in the business plan. As you write, remember that this isn't just homework that you do and then file away. This is a living and evolving document that will guide you through the steps of building and expanding your business. Refer to it when you're not sure of an important decision, need help in deciding the next step, and in evaluating the success of your plan.

To create your business plan, write down the following:

1. What is your business? Define your product or service. Include features that set your business apart from others. Many business experts recommend including a mission statement.

2. Market Analysis: Who are the people or businesses that are going to buy your products or services?

3. Competition: Who are your competitors? Who's offering what you offer? Who do they target? What are their strengths and weaknesses? How will you do better or how will you be different?

4. Management: If you're a solo entrepreneur, you're the management. If you have a partnership, the management team is the two of you. In this section, outline your skills and expertise, education and certifications as they relate to your new business.

5. Operations: How are you going to make all these ideas a reality? What are the marketing strategies and day-to-day operations that are going to create a profitable business?

6. Financials: This is where you outline your expenses and projected earnings for each month for the next twelve months.

7. Appendix: Include any information that doesn't fit into the above categories, including intellectual property protection, logos, contracts, and other business-related items.

Plan for Work-at-Home Success

1. Research your business idea, target market, and competition.

2. Determine the expenses related to your business and calculate potential income.

3. Write your business plan.

CHAPTER TWENTY

The Marketing Plan

A FEW YEARS AGO, I WAS TALKING WITH A MAN who wanted to make money from home so he could quit his truck-driving job and spend more time with his family. He contacted me about a business opportunity, but after hearing the details, determined it wasn't for him. He then told me that he was building a website that would make money 24/7. I smiled and wished him luck; however, I suspect he's still driving a truck.

Why? Because even if you're open twenty-four hours a day, seven days a week, no one will buy from you if they can't find you. With over 100 million websites online today, all competing for visitors, the chances of his website making money are nil without marketing.

It's my opinion that most businesses fail because of ineffective or nonexistent marketing. Marketing isn't always fun. Some marketing requires money with no guarantee of a return on the investment. Creating marketing systems can take time.

And with all the different marketing ideas and strategies available, it can get overwhelming to learn and implement them all. No wonder people don't market their businesses.

The good news is that marketing can be fun and affordable. Further, you don't have to implement every single idea you come across. In the next chapters, you'll be introduced to a variety of marketing strategies, from which you need to pick just a few to implement.

The Three Secrets to Marketing Success

Like many other aspects of the work-at-home topic, marketing can be made more difficult than it is. This chapter is going to detail important components of successful marketing; however, if you start to feel lost or overwhelmed, you can easily narrow successful marketing down to the following three secrets:

- Identify a target market.
- Create a message about your business that *speaks* to your target market.
- Put your message in front of the target market.

Identify a Target Market

A target market is a group of people who want or need what you're selling. To identify these people, start by answering the following questions:

1. What does your product or service do and how does it help people?

2. What are the features and benefits of your product or service?

3. What sorts of people want or need the benefits your product or service provides?

If you're thinking that everyone can benefit from your products, go ahead and write that down, but your next step will be to identify target groups within the larger group of everyone. Today, generic, one-size-fits-all marketing isn't effective. Instead, people are responding to marketing tactics that speak directly to them. The only way to do that is to identify these various groups. For example, everyone, or at least a whole lot of people, would like to work at home. But within this large group of people are distinctive subsets of people such as students, women, moms, dads, men, unemployed, disabled, disenfranchised, retired, and about-to-be retired. They all want to work at home, but for different reasons, and they'll respond better to ads that address their specific needs and desires.

You can have more than one target market, so don't feel like you'll be missing out by zeroing in on a specific group.

Create a Message That Speaks to Your Target Market

To create a message that is compelling to your target market, you need to understand a little bit about them.

- What are they interested in?
- What motivates them?
- What are some of their fears?

You'll want to answer these questions for each target group of people you've identified above. For example, in working at home, moms are usually interested in being home with children, whereas baby boomers are interested in having a secure retirement.

The point is that each group of people has their own interests, needs, and fears. Further, they all have their own language and values. By writing marketing materials that speak directly to them, using their language and tapping into their needs and desires, you're more likely to get a response than with generic advertising.

This can be better illustrated with an example. There is a large population of people who want to lose weight. We can run an ad that says: *"Lose Weight Today! Revolutionary herbal supplement allows you to eat whatever you want."* It's not bad, but let's focus on specific target markets. Who specifically wants to lose weight?

- Women that just had babies?
- Overweight people diagnosed with diabetes?

And why do people want to lose weight?

- To look sexy?
- To live longer?

What's important to them?

- Their time?
- Their health?

Your ads should reflect the answers to the above questions:

"Moms! Lose weight today! Revolutionary herbal supplement makes losing weight simple and safe!"

"Look sexy in two weeks! You'll have to beat the men off with a stick once you achieve your perfect body with this revolutionary herbal supplement."

"Live to be 100+! Ancient herbal supplement is proven to help you lose weight, lower cholesterol, and increase energy."

Each of these ads are promoting the same product, but have targeted the message to specific groups.

Put Your Message in Front of Your Target Market

Now we need to put your message in front of the people it's directed to. To do this, you need to know where they are.

■ Where does your market hang out?
■ What magazines do they read?
■ What groups do they belong to?
■ What websites do they visit?

These are the places you'll want to put your message. In the weight-loss example, we could run the mom-oriented ad in parenting magazines or offer a free weight-loss workshop to a moms group.

The Marketing Plan

Just like the business plan, the marketing plan is the road map to keeping your business in front of your target market. It outlines the details of your product or service, the ideal customer, and a handful of ideas on what you're going to do to reach them.

Do You Have USP?

In 2006, Rhonda Byrne released a video and book called *The Secret* that revealed "the secret to everything—joy, health, money, relationships, love, happiness . . . everything you've ever wanted." Marketed as a conspiracy by historic leaders to keep "The Secret" hidden, but now revealed to you, the book and video took the world by storm. Oprah devoted two episodes of her talk show to the principals of *The Secret*, and to date, millions of the book and video have sold.

However, there is no secret. In fact, if you've read anything by Napoleon Hill, Dale Carnegie, Zig Ziglar, Jack Canfield, Wallace D. Wattles, or Joe Vitale, you already know the principles of

The Secret. But Rhonda Byrne was able to repackage and market her version of the concepts in a way that made it seem not just new, but as compelling as the conspiracy presented in *The Da Vinci Code.* Whether you believe in *The Secret* or not, it's a perfect example of creating a Unique Selling Proposition (USP).

When you go shopping, whether it's for a car or macaroni or a pair of socks, you have dozens of brands to choose from. Even this book was likely next to other work-at-home-related books. So what set this book apart from the others you could have chosen? Was it that it was geared toward women? Or that it included telecommuting information? Or the cover was more interesting? Your decision to buy is related to something unique or different offered by the brand you bought. It could be price, size, or color. But there was something that made you choose one item over the other.

As you market your business, you'll need to create a uniqueness that sets you apart from the others as well. You don't need to be the fastest, brightest, or the cheapest. You just need to be different in an appealing way. This is your USP.

Developing a USP sounds easy, but because it's so important, it can actually be difficult. A USP needs to identify all the great things about your business in the smallest number of words, so you can easily convey it to your customers whether you're talking to them, handing them a business card, running a classified ad, or posting a comment on an online message board. Your USP needs to have the following components:

Customer benefit: This is not a feature such as disk brakes; it's an aspect of your feature that your customer can see herself benefiting from, such as being able to avoid a child who runs into the street in front of your car.

Proof that it works: What is it about you that makes your product or service a better choice? This goes to credibility. Why should a customer trust that your product will provide the benefits you say it will?

Uniqueness: This is what makes you stand apart from the crowd. What do you offer that others don't? What is different about you and your business from all the other choices your customer has?

Always keep your customer in mind when developing your USP. The fact that you're faster or better means nothing to your customer. Receiving same-day service (faster) that's guaranteed to exceed your expectations (better) means something.

The Art of Copywriting

More than anything, the words you use when you talk or write about your business can make or break your success. It's so important that many businesses pay thousands of dollars for a single marketing letter. There is a science to writing compelling marketing materials. Whether you're going to be working online or off, you'll eventually be using words to sell your business, so you're going to get a crash course in how to make sure your brochures, letters, or websites do the work you want them to do . . . make you money.

What Do You Have to Offer?

The first step to creating great copy for your marketing materials is to detail what it is you have and why it's so great.

1. What are the features? Is it fast or big? Is it efficient? Does it fill a need not yet filled by anything else?

2. What does it mean for your customer? Here we delve into the realm of benefits. Fast is great only if it means something to the customer, such as she'll save time. Organic is only great for someone who wants a safe or healthy product. The features (fast) that you listed in number 1 need to be translated into a benefit (save time).

3. Why are you the best source? What does your background or experience add to the credibility of your product? Do you have educational or other experience that adds to the value of what you've created?

4. What proof do you have that it's great? Nobody will take your word for how wonderful your product is. They want proof. Do you have testimonials? Have other experts used it or helped develop it?

5. What sets your product or service apart from everyone else's? It could be your expertise or it could be that you offer faster service. Maybe you have more in-depth services or a better money-back guarantee.

Be the Customer

Home-staging shows designed to help a house sell are really popular right now. One thing you hear the home stager say all the time is that the homebuyer needs to be able to see herself as the owner of the home. To do that, the homeowners have to decorate the home in a way that the buyer knows what each room is about and can feel, on a visceral level, herself living there.

The same is true when writing advertising and promotional materials. You may have a great product or service, but you need to translate those great features into something that the buyer feels she needs to have. The easiest way to do this is to put yourself in the customer's shoes and answer the question: "What's in it for me?" with "me" being the customer. "This diet is the safest and most effective," is a statement made from the business' point of view. "This diet will make you look sexy and have more energy by bikini season," is from the customer's point of view.

All forms of copywriting that are designed to sell should have the following components:

- *Words and images used by your target market:* Always, always keep your customer in mind. Remember, they don't believe you. Speak their language and solve their problems and they will buy.

- *An attention-getting headline:* In other venues (books and publicity) it's often called the "hook." Whatever you call it, it should make the customer stop and take notice.

- *WIIFM or What's in It for Me?* Promise your potential client or customer something compelling that they want.

- *Show and feel, not tell:* Use words and images that allow your potential client or customer to feel what it would be like to attain what you promise. Using the word "you" is a start, but you also want to expand on how your benefits can make their lives better. They should be able to picture and experience themselves thinner, smarter, richer, or whatever you've promised.

- *Stand out from the crowd:* Highlight your unique selling proposition (USP); how you're different from all the others who sell what you sell.

- *Prove it:* Let your customers see how your product has helped others. This can be done through testimonials. Other methods include scientific research, awards, and special recognition.

- *Why you?* This is where you establish your credibility as an expert or the credibility of experts that are involved with you.

- *Show the value:* If you aren't the least expensive, why should someone pay your price if they can pay less elsewhere? If you don't offer as many services, why should they choose you over a full-service business?

- *Tell 'em what to do:* People aren't mind readers. End your copy with a call to action that tells people what to do. Click here to buy now. Call for more details. Get your free doo-dad by mailing this card back today.

- *Offer safe sales:* A money-back guarantee is necessary to ensure top sales. People are leery of businesses that don't back their own product or service with a risk-free guaran-tee. Make it safe for your customers to buy. Create a return or refund policy that tips the scale in your favor.

Oh yeah . . . one more thing: If you're using a sales letter, end with a post script (P.S.) that reiterates the promise and the guarantee. The post script is your last chance to show how your product will enhance the life of your prospect and how she can try it out with no risk. You want them saying, "What the heck, I've nothing to lose . . ."

LAWS OF WORK-AT-HOME SUCCESS #㉖
Marketing should always focus on benefits to the cus-tomer, not how great you or your product or service is.

Customer Service

Getting expected customer service helps maintain the status quo between the customer and the business. But poor customer ser-vice can cost a business big bucks in lost revenue, just as excep-tional customer service can lead to further sales and referrals of more customers. This is how important customer service is.

Customer service is not always easy. They don't usually say thank you or give kudos for a job well done, unless it's a job done exceptionally well. But they're quick to complain. And they have that right if you promised something but didn't deliver. However, sometimes customer complaints will seem unreasonable. I have had people ask me for refunds when I wasn't selling anything.

Regardless of the situation, customer service issues need to be responded to with a level head and a helpful attitude. This is best done by developing a customer service plan that includes:

- Providing the best service possible.
- Making it easy for customers to get in touch with you. There is nothing more frustrating than being interested in buying something but not being able to find an e-mail or phone number to ask a question. People will look elsewhere to find what they need.
- Quick and professional response to complaints, even the unreasonable ones.
- Being helpful when you can. Even if people complain about things you have no control over, still offer help and support.
- Apologize and make restitution when needed. There will come a time that you will be at fault. Own up to it and make it better.

Putting It all Together

There are so many different marketing tactics that it can get overwhelming to implement a marketing plan. I use a calendar to organize my marketing activities. For example, the first and third week of every month I write and distribute articles to other websites. The second week of each month I send a press release related to an event I have planned for the following month. Mondays I post on my blogs. I try to blog Wednesdays and Fridays as well. Every Friday I send a newsletter to a list of people who sign up at my website. These are all marketing activities.

To create your own marketing plan and calendar:

1. Identify marketing strategies you will be using from the next two chapters.

2. Use a calendar or planner to schedule the activities you will do. Make sure you have at least one marketing activity every day (except on your days off).

3. Keep a list or folder of ideas for articles, press releases, or blog posts so you always have something to create when you need it.

4. Evaluate your plan. Is your marketing working? Are you able to meet your marketing deadlines?

Offline Versus Online Marketing

I have divided the offline and online marketing information into two separate chapters; however, that doesn't mean you should choose one method over the other. In fact, regardless of where your business is primarily located (online or off), you should have both online and offline marketing strategies. Every business should have a website and every website should be listed on your business card and other materials. So read and implement strategies from both chapters.

Plan for Work-at-Home Success

1. Identify your USP.

2. List the features and corresponding benefits of your products or services.

3. Identify your target market.

4. Create your message.

5. Find out where your target market hangs out.

6. Read the marketing chapters and make a marketing plan and calendar.

CHAPTER TWENTY-ONE

Marketing Unplugged

YOU'VE GOT YOUR BUSINESS PLAN, PERMITS, AND YOU'RE READY TO GO. Now what? Now you need to tell people about your business.

Marketing is one area that beginning home-based business owners fail to truly grasp the importance of. Without marketing, you don't have customers and therefore you don't have an income. But where do you start? Run an ad? Send a press release? Give away coupons? Marketing and business books are full of ideas, but it can get overwhelming to decide which to implement and how to stay organized while managing several marketing campaigns.

In this chapter, you will find many great marketing ideas. To help you implement them, I have listed them in an order based on ease of application, effectiveness, and affordability. Remember that you don't have to use every single idea presented; but you do want to select several offline and online (next chapter) tactics. Further, marketing isn't something you do once. Make time each day to do at least one thing to get your business' name out into the world.

Six Degrees of Separation

You don't need to be Kevin Bacon to take advantage of the six degrees of separation. People prefer to do business with people they know and trust. They'll also accept referrals from people they know and trust. Utilizing your network of contacts is one of the most effective and least expensive ways to jump-start your business.

The best way to activate the six degrees is to tell people you know about your business, and to give them ways to tell others about your business. This can be uncomfortable. I know it was for me. I didn't want to tell my friends and family I was working at home. They might laugh or question the wisdom of leaving my job. But word-of-mouth marketing, starting with people who know you, is too effective not to use. And did I mention it's free?

There are a variety of ways to notify your network of contacts about your business including:

Mentioning it in the course of a conversation. You don't need to give a sales pitch. Instead, say, "I'm really excited. I finally started a (insert your business here) business that I've wanted to do." Usually that's enough to have your friend or family ask you about it. Go with the flow without worrying about directing the conversation. If your friend wants to know more, she'll ask. If not, she won't and you can talk about something else.

Sending an announcement or special offer just for friends and family. Send your network of friends and family a note about your grand opening with a discount for being one of the first to support you.

Asking your friends and family to give you referrals or at least keep you in mind. How many times have you recommended a book, movie, or restaurant? Your friends can do the same for you and your business. I refer people to businesses and resources all the time. I've done it often throughout this book.

Networking with others. Expand your sphere of influence by participating in networking events. Don't be afraid to make new friends, especially if they appear to be in your target marketing group. Have a business card, your USP, and smile. You never know where it can lead.

LAWS OF WORK-AT-HOME SUCCESS #㉗

Contacting people you know and who know you is one of the fastest, most effective, and affordable ways to jump-start your business.

The Elevator Pitch

"So, what do you do?" Can you answer that question smoothly, accurately, and with enough pizzazz that the person asking you the question will want to know more? The elevator pitch is a short, compelling description of what you do. The easiest way to create your elevator pitch is to go back to your USP, as the pitch needs to address the same issues: who are you, what do you do (what problem do you solve), and why are you different? It needs to be short and snappy, and shouldn't sound like a pitch. To create your pitch:

1. Make a list of clever or catchy descriptions of what you do. Your lead-in to the pitch should create interest. Don't say, "I'm a landscaper." Instead say, "I'm a garden artist."

2. Add a few sentences that show how you're unique.

3. Create variations of your pitch that change based on who you're talking to. I have one pitch for moms and a slightly different one for baby boomers.

4. Finish by asking a question such as, "How can I help you?" or "Here, let me give you my card. Do you have a card I can have as well?"

Keep your pitch short so that it's easy to remember and it doesn't come off sounding like a pitch. Your elevator pitch should flow as smoothly and sincerely as saying, "I'm a doctor" or "I'm a social worker," but create much more interest.

Business Cards

Most people are too stingy with business cards. It probably has to do with the fact that they cost money and people don't want to waste them. But business cards are extremely affordable and too valuable not to give away. You can order them for free from VistaPrint.com (just pay shipping and handling) or create your own using your computer, printer, and business card paper from your local office store.

Business cards come in all shapes, sizes, and colors. You can get them printed sideways, backwards, and upside down. You can have print on both sides with pictures and different colors. This is all fine and wonderful as long as your card does what it's supposed to do: make it easy for people to get in touch with you.

Your card should have your business, your name, and contact information. You can even have a tag line (USP) or slogan to show your brand and help make you stand out. Additional bells and whistles are okay as long as they don't distract from the card's purpose. For example, a mortgage broker may want to have a payment calculation table on the back of the card. Or you can put a coupon on the back.

The trick to successful advertising with a business card is to:

- Always have some with you.
- Hand them out to anyone and everyone.
- Use them as note cards when someone asks you for information that needs to be written down.
- Give more than one so the person can pass it along to someone else who might need it.
- Litter. No, don't litter. But leave them behind wherever you go, whether it's to a restaurant, bank, gas station, etc.
- Put them in with your bill payments.
- Attach them to your products. Put them in your books, on the gift basket, or on the invoice for your services.

36 Places to Leave Your Business Card

- Doctor's office
- Dentist's office
- Obstetrician's office
- Pharmacies
- Veterinarian's office
- Mechanic's waiting room
- Dry cleaners
- Laundromat
- College campus
- Library (Check with the library before posting on its community board. Many libraries only accept information from nonprofits.)
- Hair salon
- Nail salon
- Tanning salons
- Video stores

- Pet stores
- Temporary Staff offices
- Tax Preparation office
- Insurance office
- Realtor's office
- Banks
- ATMs
- Mortgage offices
- Restaurants, diners, cafes
- Grocery store bulletin boards
- Health stores
- Convenience store bulletin boards
- Gas stations (on the pump)
- Day care centers
- Retirement homes
- Dance studios
- Computer stores
- Print shops
- Salespeople at any store
- Park benches
- Bus stop
- Wherever there is a waiting room

Press Releases

So far we've covered ideas that are fast and easy to implement. Press releases require a little more work, but have the potential to launch your business quickly. Press releases are short news stories that provide the who, what, when, where, why, and how of your business. They offer the perfect opportunity to showcase your expertise, brag, and announce news. Press-release topics should be newsworthy, such as:

- Announcing the opening of your business
- Changes in your business such as hiring new staff
- Special events such as sales
- New products
- Anniversaries
- Information about industry trends
- Human-interest stories
- News with tie to holidays or current events
- Solutions to common problems

Many publicity experts recommend having press releases or publicity materials distributed monthly, but it can be a challenge to invent news month after month. One way is to keep abreast of current events, tying your business with happenings in the world. Another option is to get *Chase's Calendar of Events* or a similar book that provides information about unusual events throughout the year. For example, did you know that August 8 is National Underwear Day? I'm not sure how you can incorporate that into your PR plans, but the book (or CD) provides thousands of other wacky, unusual, and even poignant events.

Press releases need to make the maximum impression with just a few hundred words. It should include:

- *An attention-getting headline.* Like other forms of marketing, a strong, catchy headline will keep the editor reading. "Local woman celebrates telecommuting week," isn't as interesting as "Local Mom trades her pantyhose for pajamas to celebrate National Telecommuter Appreciation Week!"
- *A compelling opening paragraph.* Press releases are about the who, what, when, where, why, and how of your business, but you want to deliver the information in a creative or clever manner. "Leslie Truex is a work-at-home mom

planning to celebrate National Telecommuter Week," is dry and uninteresting. "Leslie Truex, AKA The Pajama Mama, didn't leave her traditional job because she didn't like the work. She left because she didn't like the uniform," is catchier.

■ *Details of the event.* The next few paragraphs provide the details of the event or news you want to publicize in a clear, concise manner. Be brief and to the point.

■ *Statistics, facts, quotes, tips, and lists when appropriate* to provide support to your news and oomph to your press release.

The Press-Release Format

If your press release needs to appear in the press by a specific date, indicate that at the top of the page. Or simply put, "For Immediate Release." Open the press release with a title (headline). Bold the title, but don't use all caps. The first line begins with the city, state, and date, followed by your opening sentences. The body should be double-spaced and preferably no longer than one page. Add details you want the readers of the article or interviewer to know about, such as how to get more information. End the press release with "###" or "-30-" to let the editor or reporter know they've reached the end of the press release. Finally, don't forget your contact information so the editor or reporter can get back to you.

Snail Mail Versus E-mail

Today, many media outlets accept e-mailed press releases. It's an ideal way to get your press release out quickly while also saving on postage. However, you should check with the media source to make sure it accepts e-mail press releases. Other tips for sending your press release include:

■ *Targeting appropriate media outlets.* One of the biggest complaints made by editors and producers is that they receive news releases on topics they don't cover.

■ *Get the release into the right hands.* I have found this the biggest challenge. Is my news a community event or business news? Does it go to the editor or the newsroom? Fortunately, a little leg work can help. Visit the media outlet's website or call them to find out who your press release should be directed to. Also ask if that person accepts e-mail press releases.

■ *Get it read.* If you're e-mailing your press release, use an attention-grabbing subject for the e-mail. I like to use the title (headline) of my press release. You don't want to mislead the editor, but you do want to have something that will stand out from the other e-mail.

■ *Help the editor or producer do their job by ensuring your release is newsworthy, and include any references that can help them do their job.* For example, if your news item uses statistics or survey results, provide the information to access the statistics and results themselves.

■ *Be accurate.* If you're sending details or specific facts, check that they're right. Inaccurate information will negatively impact your credibility.

■ *Think locally and globally.* It would be nice to be on *Oprah* or interviewed for *People* magazine, but as you can imagine, unless your story is truly unique, the odds of getting attention from these sources is small. Start with your local daily and weekly newspapers, as well as local news stations. Also contact media outlets that target your market. If you have a fabulous product for moms, send your information to regional and national parenting magazines. If your product will help baby boomers live longer, more active lives, send your press release to trade and consumer magazines that baby boomers read.

Creating a Media List

As you gather the names and contact information of media people, add them to a database. This will make it easier to send them releases in the future. Every six months or so, contact the media outlet to verify that the person is still there and is the correct person to contact. People come and go and won't always direct your release to the right person.

Articles

Writing articles is a fantastic way to promote your business as well as position yourself as an expert in your field. Not only that, but it's free and if you show real talent, you could also get paid. To write and submit articles:

1. Identify media markets that your target market reads. These could be newspapers (dailies, weeklies, etc.), business journals, trade journals, alumni magazines, or newsletters.

2. Visit your local bookstore or newsstand to see what types of newspapers and magazines exist that fit your market. *Writer's Digest* puts out a book each year that lists thousands of writing markets. Or you can access their database online at *www.writersmarket.com*.

3. Determine the type of article you'd like to write. Some ideas include op-ed pieces, columns, feature stories, how-to information, news and trends, or personal experience essays.

4. Fit your article type to the media outlet you've chosen. If you want to write a personal essay, check the paper or magazine to make sure it accepts essays.

5. Outline your article. You don't have to use the roman numerals as you were taught in middle school, but you should get the basic ideas and structure of your article outlined before

you start writing. A basic article will have an opening, a couple of paragraphs that cover a specific idea, and a closing.

6. Write a piece that stands out from the crowd. While you don't want to write an ad, you do want to use some concepts from copywriting such as having a hook or headline that grabs the reader's attention.

7. Be personable but not too informal. Many experts suggest writing how you talk. This can be a helpful tactic to get your ideas out onto the page. However, you want to be careful about being too informal. You'd be surprised at how many articles I come across using "you know" and other forms of expression that should be limited to spoken language.

8. Check your article for spelling and grammar errors. Remember, the idea is to position yourself as an expert, so you can't have glaring errors that will distract from your piece.

9. Put your writing aside for a night.

10. Reread it out loud. This will help you identify errors, as well as areas of the article that don't flow well or make sense.

11. Include information about you and your business in a byline that includes your name and contact information. Many publications allow you to include a small blurb about you and your business. If so, this is a great place to share your accomplishments or provide a free offer.

12. Save samples of your writing. Whenever your article appears, get a copy to use in other marketing materials such as your media kit.

Classified Ads

Fortunes have been made through small $20 ads. When placing ads, check with the news source that your offer doesn't violate its ad policy. For example, some papers don't allow business opportunity ads.

Consider all papers in your area such as the weeklies and community papers. Check online at sites like My Classified Ads (*www.myclassifiedads.net*) to place ads outside your local area.

Flyers

Some people have fantastic responses with flyers and others tell me it is a waste of time. Because it involves little time and expense, it may be worth trying. Use your computer word-processing or desktop-publishing program to create professional-looking flyers. Make them in black and white, but print them on durable colored paper. Studies suggest that bright orange attracts viewers.

Review the copywriting section for details on creating attention-grabbing copy to get your prospects to take action. Also, use tear tabs on the flyer. Many word-processing programs can fill in your name, website, phone number and other contact information at the bottom of the page. Then potential clients can simply tear the information off, leaving the rest of the flyer intact.

Coupons

Who doesn't want to save money? Coupons are a great way to entice new customers to try your product or service. Once they try, the value and service will keep them coming back. You can run a coupon as part of an ad, send them in mailers, or leave them like drop cards at area businesses.

For coupons to work, they need to offer a large enough discount to make it worth the time and effort for a potential customer to redeem. If your client has to jump through hoops, it needs to be worth their time and hassle to do it.

Contests

Everyone loves to be a winner. Contests are an effective and creative way to help build your database of potential customers by giving them the chance to win something in exchange for their information. Many women in the direct-sales of cosmetics use this method to offer free makeovers. They leave boxes with entry forms at nail salons or other stores that women frequent.

If the prize if really large, you can gain more recognition and more registrants by sending a press release to the media about your contest.

It's important to note that there are laws that govern contests and sweepstakes. Include information in the fine print that explains:

- *How to enter.* Is a purchase necessary? Is there any limitation such as age or geographical location?
- *Details on the prize(s).*
- *Disclaimer.* Since you're running a business promotion, you may want to use the winner's name and photograph in publicity materials. You need to let entrants know that by entering the contest they are giving you the right to use their name and information in advertising campaigns.
- *Liability protections.* Have a clause that waives your liability for injury or damage experienced by the winner.
- *Rules.* Can people enter more than once? Can they only have a set number of entries per day? Do they need to be present to win? Where can they mail entries?

The federal government and individual states each have laws governing contests. It will be worth having a chat with your lawyer before running your contest to ensure you're not breaking any rules.

Direct-Response Marketing

Did you check your mail today? Did you get any credit card applications, donation requests, or offers of the next best thing?

Most unsolicited mail ends up in the garbage; however, I'm going to encourage you to read it, as it can be a tool to teach you about direct-response marketing.

Sending direct mail to the right person at the right time can make you rich, but it could also break the bank. Mailing lists (which are rented, not bought) and postage can send a single direct-mail campaign's costs into the thousands of dollars. For a successful direct-mail campaign you'll need:

A professionally written mail piece. I covered copywriting in the last chapter, but unless you truly understand copywriting, consider hiring someone. There is a science to the sales letter and you don't want to spend money on a list and postage for a letter that isn't going to get results.

A targeted list. You can rent lists targeted to specific groups by demographics, interest, and location. Again, the goal is to get the right message (your offer) to the right group (people who want what you've got). The list is rented and can only be used once. You can add only those people who respond to your offer to your permanent database.

Bulk mail permit. Fortunately, you don't have to pay the full postage price for mailing in bulk. The U.S. Postal Service will provide you with discounted mailing prices when you mail more than 200 pieces. You have to sort them by zip code and prepare them to the post office's specifications. To send by bulk mail, the U.S. Post Office requires that you rent a postage meter and apply for a bulk mail permit. You will be given a special permit number to use in your mailing. For more information, visit *www .usps.com/businessmail101/postage/howToApply.htm.*

Advertising (Television, Radio, Print)

Advertising can be expensive, so evaluate and investigate ad opportunities carefully.

Choose ad mediums that target your market. If you sell health products, put your ads in health and wellness newspapers or magazines, instead of your regular daily newspaper.

Learn copywriting or hire someone to create professional copy. If you're using graphics, hire someone to do that as well.

Track the results so you can know if a sudden spike in sales is the result of your ad or your press release. There are several ways to track an ad, including:

- Asking people how they found you.
- Telling people they need to provide a special code and giving each ad its own code.
- Referring to specific websites or e-mail. Provide one website for the ad run in the local paper and a different website for the ad run in the health paper.

Community Involvement

Community involvement not only introduces you to potential customers, but because it usually involves acts of goodwill, you're automatically seen in a positive light. Community involvement can include volunteer work, supporting a local youth sports team, or helping fund important community services.

Public Speaking (Seminars and Workshops)

Despite what you may think, the odds of dying of stage fright are practically nil. That doesn't stop most people from dreading public speaking. Nevertheless, public speaking is a surefire way to position yourself as an expert, gain credibility, and reach more customers. Further, if you turn out to be good at it, it can be another income source for you.

You don't have to start your public speaking career talking to thousands or even hundreds of people. The best starting point for a beginning speaker is in her own back yard at places like adult education centers, service clubs, associations, and organizations. Use your phone book, Chamber of Commerce, and library to find a list of local groups that have meetings and could use a speaker.

In developing your speech, remember the rules of good marketing:

- Create an interesting title.
- Know who you're talking to.
- Provide useful information in an organized manner that shows you know your business.
- Give them an offer. Your speech should not be a sales talk, but you can offer a discount or a giveaway to participants.

For more help on developing your speaking skills and overcoming fear in public speaking, visit *www.toastmasters.org*.

Sales

Sales has to be one of the scariest words on earth, second only to tax audit or maybe network marketing. And it's no wonder. We've all been the victim of pushy salespeople. And we know how telemarketers are treated. Why would we want to put ourselves in a position to get yelled at or hung up on? The good news is that sales doesn't have to be the cold, in your face, pressure and hype that it's often associated with.

Sales isn't about coercion as it's often depicted. It's about persuasion, education, and recommendation. When was the last time you recommended a great book and included all sorts of reasons why it should be read? That's sales.

There are three basic ways to do sales. One way we've already covered in copywriting and items that involve writing (brochures, flyers, ads, etc.). The other two are usually the ones that freak people out. They are person-to-person and phone sales. But never fear because I'm going to give you a great nine-step plan to achieving sales success.

Step One: Let the prospect reveal himself. I have a mentor who says that I could put him in any city in the U.S. or Canada with a phone book and phone and he could build a successful business. I believe it. He is one of those "salesmen." But even people who can cold call without a moment's hesitation would rather talk with motivated buyers than uninterested prospects. My friend would rather call 100 people who said they wanted to know more about what he had than 1,000 people listed in the phone book. And the results would be about the same. So it's more effective and efficient to talk to people who want to know about what you've got. How do you do that? You do it by responding to people who have contacted you through one of your other forms of advertising and promotion.

Step Two: Qualify your prospect. I used to sell real estate. One thing I was taught early on was to qualify home buyers before showing them homes for sale. The idea is that you don't want to waste your time with people who don't have the money (or credit to get the money) to buy a house. If you were to call an agent to buy a house, the first thing she'll want to know is if you'd talked to a mortgage officer. This is a qualifying question and is designed to make sure that the potential customer is able to buy.

But you don't want to be obnoxious about qualifying people by asking them question after question regarding their financial status. In most cases, asking simple questions such as:

- What led you to contact me?
- What are you hoping to get/do/achieve?
- How soon are you looking to get/do/achieve it?

will give you the insight into the customer's desire and ability to buy what you offer.

Step Three: Talk with, not at, your prospect. I'm a concrete person. When I learn something new, I want every step laid out. When I started working on the phone, I wanted a script . . . a word-for-word outline of what I was supposed to say. But we all know that talking from a script is ineffective. You probably had a call today that used the right words, but clearly wasn't interested in your response. "Hello Mrs. Truex how are you. It's such an awful day in Houston today. How is it in Virginia? Blah, blah, blah . . ."

There is a place for scripts, but I prefer bulleted lists to keep me on track with my presentation and still allow me to listen and converse with the customer. By doing so, I build rapport and can use my product or service to solve their problems. "Hello Mrs. Truex. This is Leslie from ABC Inc. I'm getting back to you on your request for information about my gadget. Have I caught you at a good time?" You'll notice that by contacting someone who asked me for information, I'm already more likely to have their interest. But I also recognize that I may be calling at a bad time. If they say now is not a good time, I ask when a better time would be and get off the phone. I'm not a telemarketer. If it is a good time, I use my script to guide me through the process of qualifying them, learning what they want and need, and educating them about how I can help.

Step Four: Take the "No" and move on. How do you feel when you tell the telemarketer, "I'm not interested," and she proceeds to say, "I understand, but did you know . . ." If you haven't hung up already, the telemarketer will continue to use this line in an attempt to browbeat you into buying. In fact, telemarketers are evaluated on whether or not they accept your no or keep on selling. Presumably, the more they ignore you, the better their boss likes them. But you don't want to be a telemarketer. When someone says no, take it as a no.

Diehard salespeople will likely disagree. They work under the premise that buyers are liars (not a very good frame of mind to start the sales process to begin with). Instead, they keep talking and when that doesn't work, they turn a bit nasty. I have been told I was ruining my child's future by not buying a time-share, and just the other day, I told someone I wasn't interested in his program and he said, "You're not who I want to work with," as if I was going to change my mind and say, "Oh please work with me."

Step Five: This may seem contradictory, but just because you get a no today, doesn't mean you'll always get a no. Timing is a factor in sales. I've made sales to people months, even years, after the original pitch. If I had continued to ignore them or annoy them, that future sale would never have occurred. Instead, take the no, but allow for follow-up.

Step Six: Follow-up. I love the line, "The fortune is in the follow-up." By staying in touch with your potential clients (with their permission of course), you can build credibility and a relationship, thereby making them feel better about buying from you when the time is right for them.

If a client says no, ask if you can put them on your mailing (or e-mailing) list to send them periodic information and/or special offers. I find most people say yes because they feel bad about the no and relieved you aren't going to harass them any further. Send them a thank-you note (by snail mail or e-mail) and add them to your e-mail or mailing list. Then don't forget to send them information every now and then.

If a client doesn't say no but doesn't say yes either, follow-up will be key. Determine what the problem is. Is it timing? Do they need more information? Is someone else involved in the decision? Whatever the reason, follow up with the information to move the sale forward.

Step Seven: Ask for the sale. In an attempt to not be pushy, many people are afraid to ask for the sale. Part of the problem is the way sales experts suggest you make the sale. "So Mrs. Smith, shall I put you down for two or three . . . ?" At the same time, buyers, except on rare occasions, aren't going to jump out of their chair and say, "Sell me those!" You have to ask for the sale. There are a variety of low-pressure ways to do this. One is to ask for feedback on their level of interest in buying. "Mrs. Smith, on a scale of one to five, with one being this isn't the product for you and five being you're ready to purchase now, what would you rate your level of interest in buying [insert your product here]?" If Mrs. Smith says, "Five," you have a sale. If she says, "One," you don't. If she gives another number, she needs more information to make a decision.

Step Eight: Treat objections as questions, not no's. An objection isn't a no, it's a potential yes. To deal with objections, anticipate what they might be, such as "The price seems high" or "I don't have the time." Then come up with a question to address their objection. "If price wasn't a factor, would you buy?" If they say yes, then you have someone who is interested, but not enough to spend what it costs. Your job then is to help them see the value. Will it save them money? Is there a payment plan?

Step Nine: Don't talk too much. Less really is more in the sales process. If your prospects seek you out and ask for information, your job is to help them through the process of determining that your product or service will fix their problems or meet their needs. To do this, you have to ask questions and let them tell you what they need. You share information only as it relates to helping them get what they want using your product.

More Sales Tips

In a phone contact, always let the person know why you're calling and how you got their name. Also ask if it's a good time to talk. If it's not, make an appointment for another time and get off the phone.

For the person in sales, have visuals, but don't rely on them. Keep the process a conversation and not a presentation. Use visuals only when needed to make a point.

Smile and make eye contact.

Respect your prospect's time. Keep your meeting to thirty minutes or less.

Plan for Work-at-Home Success

1. Make a list of people you know or who know you and find a way to let them know about your new venture.

2. Develop your elevator pitch.

3. Buy or create your own business card and generously give them away.

4. Write a press release about your new business.

5. Identify two or three other offline marketing strategies that you can use on a regular basis.

CHAPTER TWENTY-TWO

Marketing Online

WHETHER OR NOT YOU PLAN TO SELL YOUR GOODS OR SERVICES ONLINE, you should have an online presence. Your competition will, and it will look like you're stuck in the dark ages if you don't.

I have again organized the marketing strategies here based on ease of implementation, efficiency, and cost effectiveness.

Six Degrees Again . . .

Even in the virtual world, you know and are in contact with people who can help you with your business. One of the fastest and least expensive ways to build your business is by letting these people know what you're up to using the methods below:

- *E-mail announcement:* In the last chapter, I suggested that you tell your friends and family about your business through casual conversation or by sending them a grand opening announcement. This can be done online through e-mail as well.

■ *Signature lines:* These lines of text with a website or blog URL are like a business card attached to your e-mail. The most effective signature lines include a free offer or some other compelling information to get them to go to your website. Include a signature line in all your e-mail.

■ *Forums and discussion groups:* These online clubs offer a great way to increase your credibility and expert status, as well as to network with others. If you already belong to online groups, start by adding your signature line to all your posts, if it's allowed. You don't need to post an ad (most groups don't allow ads anyway), but you can often include your information as part of your signature. When you participate in groups, always offer helpful information and compelling (not controversial) conversation.

■ *Social networking:* MySpace.com and Facebook.com are two examples of online social networks. They are a step beyond discussion forums because they allow much more than discussion. You get your own web page, where you can outline your business and interests and interact with your network of friends. Your friends can comment on your page and visa versa, creating opportunities to expose your business to other potential friends (six degrees at work). However, social networking can be time consuming and unproductive if you don't have a plan.

Search Engines

One goal most online entrepreneurs strive to achieve is top ranking in a search engine. This is truly a feat. Whether or not you reach number #1 or #20, getting your website on the search engines is important to your success.

Several search engines automatically crawl the web searching for sites to add to its database. However, you can speed things up by submitting your website or blog information directly. Submitting your website to search engines is relatively easy; getting a good ranking (having your page show up near the top of the search results) is harder. There is a science to search engine optimization (SEO) that involves having good keywords in the meta tags and body of your website pages (see chapter on website building for more information), a site map (a page listing all the pages of your website), and link popularity (the number of other sites that link to yours).

There are services and software that you can buy to submit your website to thousands of search engines and directories; however, for the most part, it's a waste of money. The majority of web surfers use one of the resources listed below to search the web. Just visit the link, give your website information, and click "Submit."

Google *www.google.com/addurl.html*

Yahoo *https://siteexplorer.search.yahoo.com/submit*

MSN *http://search.msn.com/docs/submit.aspx*

AltaVista: *http://addurl.altavista.com/addurl/new*

Scrub the Web *www.scrubtheweb.com/addurl.html*

Open Directory *www.dmoz.org/add.html* (Other engines and directories such as AOL and Yahoo use Open Directory's data to list on their resources).

LAWS OF WORK-AT-HOME SUCCESS #28
Use your keywords in all of your online marketing strategies to improve search-engine ranking and increase website traffic.

E-mail and Autoresponders

E-mail is a blessing and a curse to online marketers. It's a fantastic way to stay in touch with customers, build relationships, and create credibility. In fact, there is a saying that the list (of e-mails) is gold. On the other hand, people are overwhelmed and fed up with e-mails they don't have time to read or don't want to receive.

The most successful (read profitable) e-mail list will be the one you develop yourself. To build an e-mail list, you need to determine why you want the list. Is it to help sell your products? Is it to promote affiliate programs? Is it simply for informational purposes? The most common list uses are:

■ *Newsletters:* Many business owners use a weekly, bi-weekly, or monthly newsletter to keep customers up to date on trends, issues, and specials. Newsletters consist of articles, reviews, specials, advertising, and even a personal note from the publisher.

■ *Lead capture:* This is used a great deal in direct-selling businesses that recruit other representatives. A person who is interested in getting more information about the company or the products can fill in a form that is sent to the site owner. The site owner can e-mail or even call the lead to follow up. The most successful lead capture sites offer a series of follow-up e-mails that provide information about the company and products.

■ *Tips and announcements:* Many years ago I had created an e-mail list that received a work-at-home job of the day. Some websites specialize in finding special savings in everything from baby stuff to wholesale items for resale. A mortgage person could use a tip and announcement e-mail list to send out interest rates and current news on the mortgage industry.

■ *Reports:* A report is a short document that informs or educates your prospect on something related to your business. If you have a health and wellness business, you can offer a free report about toxins in the home or easy ways to exercise. The report can be a marketing tool in itself, referring people back to your product or services.

■ *E-courses:* An e-course (e-mail course) allows you to share just enough information to let people know you are knowledgeable and credible to entice them to buy your products.

■ *Registration:* Even if you have a free website, you can ask people to register to access the information on your website. This gives you the opportunity to keep them informed of changes to the member's area as well as send special announcements or reviews.

All these options can help you create a targeted list of people's e-mails that you can use to promote your products or services. While you never want to send ad after ad, you can have advertising, recommend affiliate products, and promote your own products and services. As long as your subscribers find your e-mails informative or entertaining, they will continue to receive them.

But there are rules.

Rule Number 1: Create double opt-in lists. When someone inputs their name and e-mail into a form and hits the "submit" button, they have opted-in to receive e-mail from that site. Unfortunately, there are spammers that will input people's names who don't want to be on a list. Therefore, you want to send a confirmation e-mail asking the person to confirm that she wants to be on the list. This is double opt-in because they have to say yes twice. If you're given the choice, always go with double opt-in lists to avoid getting accused of spamming. Most e-mail list services provide for double opt-in mailing lists.

Rule Number 2: Know why you're e-mailing. Are you sending your weekly newsletter? Do you have a special offer? Is it part of an e-course or a free report? You need a good reason to send an e-mail, and that reason should be compelling to the recipient.

Rule Number 3: Don't over e-mail. People are inundated with e-mail, so you don't want to overdo it by e-mailing too often. Your e-mailing schedule depends on the answer to number one. If you're e-mailing a tip of the day, then you'll send an e-mail every day. A newsletter is usually e-mailed once a week or once a month. You want to have enough mailings to keep your name and business known to your prospects, but not so much that they decide they're getting too much e-mail and unsubscribe.

Rule Number 4: Make your subject line compelling and accurate. A subject line is like a headline in advertising. It needs to create interest so that the recipient will open it. However, it must accurately describe what's in the e-mail. Using scare tactics or other gimmicks that don't directly relate to the e-mail is a violation of the CAN-SPAM law. Plus, it annoys people, and annoyed people won't want to do business with you.

Rule Number 5: Include your contact information (including address) in the e-mail. This is important for two reasons. One is that you want your prospect to be able to get in touch with you about your offer or information. Second, it is required by law.

Rule Number 6: Let subscribers know how they can get off your list. This is another important requirement to avoid being labeled a spammer. Many list services automatically have a link that people can use to unsubscribe. If you don't have this, give directions on how people can be removed from your list. And be sure to remove them if they ask.

CAN-SPAM Law

In January 2004, the Controlling the Assault of Non-Solicited Pornography and Marketing Act (known as the CAN-SPAM Act of 2003) went into effect. The law outlines the rules for commercial e-mailing and penalties for spammers who ignore the rules. The rules include:

1. No false or misleading header information. This means that you have to use an e-mail account owned by you. Spammers will often input someone else's e-mail (e-mail spoofing) or a false e-mail in the "From" box. You see this commonly in phishing schemes where a spammer sends an e-mail that looks like it's from PayPal or eBay or a bank, when it's not.

2. No use of deceptive subject lines to trick people into opening the e-mail.

3. Opt-out methods are required so that recipients can unsubscribe.

4. E-mails that are advertising must be labeled as such.

5. Physical address of the sender must be included.

Fines for violating CAN-SPAM laws can be steep, up to $11,000. Plus violators can face other fines if they break advertising laws, harvest e-mails, or use another computer or network to send e-mails without permission.

To learn more, visit www.ftc.gov/bcp/edu/pubs/business/ecommerce/bus61.shtm.

The best way to send e-mail to your customers is through an autoresponder service. Autoresponders automatically send your e-mail to people who request to receive it. It can subscribe people to your newsletter, deliver your free report or e-course, and anything else that can be sent by e-mail. Further, it can deliver a series of messages over the course of days, months, even the year. Here are some examples of what e-mail autoresponders can do:

- Collect newsletter subscription, send confirmation (double-opt in) and welcome e-mail.
- Send multiple-day e-course.
- Provide training over a period of time. Training materials can be e-mailed daily or every few days depending on how you set it up.
- Send free report or other free e-goodies.

Autoresponder services are not only a convenient way to automate your e-mail, but they offer you protection as well. Most require double opt-in confirmation, supply a link for unsubscribing, and include your address, making your e-mails CAN-SPAM compliant. Further, some will do spam checks that analyze the content of your e-mail to see if subscribers' spam filters will target your e-mail for deletion.

There are a variety of autoresponder services. I use Aweber.com because at the time, it was the only one that allowed unlimited lists through one account. Now it appears that most of them, such as Getresponse.com, offer unlimited lists.

There are free autoresponder services; however, if you need reliability, I'd go with a paid service. When researching services, don't just note price, but also features such as the ability to send HTML versus text messages, templates, tracking, and importing.

Because you can lose many subscribers when you change list services, choose one that you can stay and grow with.

Newsletters or E-zines

In the previous section I mentioned newsletters as a part of e-mail marketing. Newsletters can do a great deal to show off your expertise and create relationships with potential customers. Further, they can help you make more money through advertising revenue, affiliate products, and sales of your own products and services.

Don't worry if you aren't a writer or a desktop publisher. Newsletters don't have to be long or elaborate. In fact, in today's busy world, people who read online content just want the beef—concise information they can use now. Here are some tips for a good basic newsletter:

- *Begin with a welcome message from you.* Many people share personal (not too personal) information that helps your subscribers know you better.
- *Include an article or tip list related to your topic area.* If you have a gardening business, put tips on getting the yard ready for fall or summer. If you sell health and wellness products, have an article on how to read product labels or choosing a gym. If you don't feel comfortable writing an article, you can find free reprint articles online that you can use. These articles will have links that direct readers to the author's website which means your visitors can leave your site. However, if you are in need of good content, free reprint articles are a great way to add value to your newsletter.
- *If you want to earn affiliate revenue, you can offer a special or review of the week with a link to a product.*

- *Use ads sparingly.* It's okay to have advertising, but they shouldn't take up more space than the articles.
- *Don't forget your signature line at the end.*

Free Stuff

Offering free stuff is a great way to encourage people to sign up for your newsletter or share their e-mail address for future contact. Free stuff can include:

- Reports
- E-books
- E-courses
- List of resources
- Phone consultations
- Teleseminars

Ideally, you want to create your own free product so you can build your credibility and have it be a promotional tool for your business. If you're selling gardening tools, a free report or list of the top-ten tools can highlight your knowledge and also can direct people back to your site so they can buy those ten tools.

Blogs

You've already seen how you can use a blog alone to market your business. However, it can also be used as a marketing tool for your website. Because blogs are frequently updated, they provide incentives for your visitors to keep coming back to see what's new. Further, search engines love blogs because they tend to be keyword rich and offer new content on a regular basis.

One of the best features of blogs is that they are free and very easy to set up. In five minutes you can have a blog set up through Blogger.com or Wordpress.com. They're also easy to update. Simply log in, type your content, and post. There's no web page building and uploading.

For blogs to be helpful marketing tools, they need to be updated frequently, at least three times a week. They also need to provide content, stories, or resources your market is interested in.

Things to post on your blog include:

- Any articles you write for your website or newsletter
- Press releases
- News and current trends
- Personal stories as they relate to your business topic
- Lists such as Top 10 lists

When you blog, you don't need to write a thesis. Short and to-the-point writing that is interesting or compelling is what blogging is all about.

Like websites, people won't read your blog if they don't know about it. Fortunately, blogs offer several great features for automatic marketing. To get your blog known:

- *Allow comments.* Comments allow visitors to post their opinions or stories about your blog post.
- *Enable trackbacks.* This allows people to add your blog post to their blog.
- *Create an RSS feed for your blog.* Most blog services and software have a feature to do this. A blog feed allows other websites and feed aggregators (software or web service that collects multiple blog feeds to showcase in one spot) to pull the information from your blog to be read by others.
- *Make it easy for visitors to subscribe and add your blog to their feed reader (aggregator).* You can make this easy by creating one-click feed subscriptions on your blog.

- *Use Google Sitemaps when you update your blog.* To do this, you need to submit the blog to Google at *www.google.com/addurl.* You'll need to wait until Google has visited your blog before proceeding. You can check that your site has been visited by visiting Google and typing "cache:http://yourblogurl" in the search box. When the site has been cached, create a Google Sitemap account at *www.google.com/webmasters/sitemaps.* Click the "Add" tab to submit your blog to Google Sitemaps.

- *Ping your blog updates.* Pinging lets other resources such as the feed aggregators know that a new post has been added. Check your blog service to see if it offers pinging. If not, you can visit Pingomatic (*www.pingomatic.com*) and use its service for free.

- *List your blog in blog directories or search engines.* The most well known is Technorati (*www.technorati.com*).

- *Network with other blogs.* Visit other blogs and post comments. Use the trackback feature to add other people's posts to your blog and comment on them.

- *Update your blog regularly.*

Link Exchange

I'll post your URL if you post mine. That is the essence of a link exchange. A link exchange allows you to tap into the traffic of other websites while doing the same for the other site. Further, because your URL is showing up on another website, link exchanges can improve your link popularity and therefore your search-engine ranking. For link exchanges to work they must have:

- Links to sites that are related to yours.
- Links to sites of good-quality. You will be judged by the company you keep, so make sure any sites that you link to have the same standards and integrity as you do.

■ A fair exchange. The links need to be easily found on both sites. Some people try to hide their partner links. Don't work with people like that.

To negotiate a link exchange:

1. Search for websites that you like and trust.

2. Create a "Links" or "Resources" page on your website and add the websites you'd like to trade links with to the page.

3. Once you have uploaded your Links page, e-mail the owners of the websites and let them know you have visited their sites and liked what they offered so much that you have added their websites to your Links page. Ask them if they would be willing to add your site to their Links page as well.

4. Make it easy for them to decide by adding a link to your site with a small blurb about your site. This will allow them to visit your site and then simply cut and paste your information onto their site.

If someone sends you a link request, always verify that your link is on the site. Also check that when clicked it goes to your website. Finally, visit the site's home page and verify that the page your link is on can be accessed. Many deceptive link partners will hide the pages or links so that no visitor to their site would be able to find your link.

Articles

Articles for online marketing can be extremely helpful. They cost nothing and take little time to create. But they deliver mass exposure and credibility, as other websites, blogs, and online newsletters need quality content and are willing to publish your work. In exchange for your free article, the publisher includes your business information so that readers can learn more about you.

While you don't need a degree in English to get your articles published online, you do need to create concise and informative articles. One of my pet peeves is the difficulty in finding articles that are well written, flow, and make sense to publish in my newsletter. Here are my tips for writing articles that will get published:

1. Outline before writing. You don't need the outline that you learned in seventh-grade English, but you do need to have a plan to keep focused on the topic.

2. Relate all ideas and concepts to your introduction. You'd be surprised at how many people have an introduction about one topic, but the body of the article is about something else.

3. Use bullets or numbered lists to keep your writing on target. Readers love lists, as they tend to be right to the point and easy to read.

4. Don't write for academics, but don't be too personable either. It's okay to write as if you are talking as long as you take out all the "you knows" and clichés. Compare, "Working at home is totally awesome. You can do what you want when you want to and nobody is looking over your shoulder. It's the best of both worlds" to "Working at home is awesome. It allows you to do the type of work you love and set your own hours." While neither are Pulitzer-winning sentences, hopefully you can see that the first sentence is too wordy, awkward, and informal.

5. Provide tips and information. People are online to get information. Give it to them.

6. Include an author bio that has a call to action. Don't simply give your name or website. Add your free giveaway or newsletter information. For example:

About the Author: Leslie Truex is a work-at-home mom who has been offering free information and resources about telecommuting and home business since 1998. Get The Jobs Online Toolkit with a subscription to her FREE newsletter at *www.workathomesuccess.com.*

7. Submit your articles everywhere you can. Visit Yahoo Groups and type in "article announcements" to see a list of groups that will share your article with other publishers. Submit it to Best Syndication, *www.bestsyndication.com*, where it will be fed to other websites and news services.

If article marketing will be a major part of your online marketing plan, consider using an article distribution service. For a fee, you can submit your article to one place that will send it to thousands of other websites and publishers. For the time it saves, it's worth the expense. At Isnare.com (*www.isnare.com*), you can buy distribution credits. This situation is ideal if you are submitting just a few articles a month. If you'll be distributing several articles a week, you can upgrade your service at Isnare. com or use ArticleMarketer.com, where you can get unlimited article submissions for one monthly price.

Press Releases

I covered all the benefits of press releases in the offline marketing chapter. In the online world, press releases offer the same benefits plus allow you to reach more markets, as many reporters use the Internet to find news stories.

Online press releases tend to be shorter than regular press releases, but still require the same organization and information.

I prefer to use the free press-release services, but if you need big exposure fast, there are paid services as well. Here is a list of a few free services you can use. Don't forget to post your press release on your website and blog.

- PRNuke.com
- USPRWire.com
- PRFree.com
- PRZoom.com
- PRLeap.com
- PRWeb.com

Joint Ventures

Joint ventures are an excellent way to supercharge your sales. A joint venture involves two or more businesses that join together to share their assets for mutual benefit. You may have a fabulous product, but a small market. Emily Entrepreneur may have a huge market (e-mail list), but nothing new to promote to it. In a joint venture, you provide the product and Emily Entrepreneur markets it to her list, and you both share in the profits. To participate in a joint venture you need to:

1. Research potential partners. Who has websites that are similar or complementary to what you offer? For example, if you have a gardening e-book and Emily Entrepreneur is a gardening consultant, she would be a good person to approach.

2. Get statistics. From the list you create in number 1, what are the statistics for those sites? What is their Google Page rank (you need Google Toolbar to see this) or Alexa rating. E-mail the owner to ask how many people are on their newsletter list and the amount of unique traffic (not hits) to the site.

3. Choose one. When you have identified a good potential joint partner, e-mail her. Let her know who you are and what you have to offer. Tell her why you chose her (give compliments) and how you think you'd both make a good fit to work together.

Be willing to send a copy of your product for free so she can review it and decide if she wants to endorse it.

4. If agreeable, work together to iron out the details, such as the profit split, how commissions will be tracked, and how commissions will be paid.

5. Work together. Your JV partner may have ideas to help boost sales. If you're using your JV partner's list, listen to her ideas, as she'll know her subscribers better than you. Be available to answer questions, and keep in touch throughout the process.

6. Pay ASAP. Establish a pay date in your contract, and then pay on time. Don't forget to include a thank you and an initiation to joint venture together again in the future.

7. Find a new partner and repeat the process again.

Advertising

Advertising your business on other websites or e-zines (online newsletters) can be effective and affordable, if you do your research. Gone are the days in which a banner ad can make you rich. To use online advertising effectively you need to:

- *Write a compelling, action-producing ad or banner graphic.*
- *Find websites or newsletters in your target market.* In my experience, small and mid-size websites and newsletters are the most affordable and have the best results over larger sites.
- *Research advertising rates and statistics.* Many websites have this information on the website. If not, contact the owner. Questions you want to ask include: How many unique visitors (not hits) does the site get a day or a month? How many newsletter subscribers are there? What are the advertising rates for various ads?
- *Avoid classified ads.* While these are the most affordable, the results aren't worth the price. I prefer a homepage ad

(ad on the main page of the site) and solo or sponsor ads in online newsletters. A solo ad is e-mailed by itself to the newsletter list, whereas the top sponsor ad is the first ad shown in the publication and is set apart from other ads.

■ *Track the ad.* You can't know if the jump in sales is related to your ad or your article if you don't track it. One way to track your ads is to add a special code after the URL for each ad, such as *www.yourdomain.com/?biz1solo*, where "biz1solo" identifies the site and type of ad you're running. You can use anything after the "?" as long as it makes sense to you. To see the results, view your website statistics. Another option is to use a tracking service that will create unique URLs for each of your ads. The service tracks how many times each URL was clicked on. There are free and paid services depending on how much information you want and how many links you need at a given time. I have used Click Audit (*www.clickaudit.com*).

Pay-Per-Click Advertising (PPC)

People make and lose fortunes every day using pay-per-click advertising. In pay-per-click (PPC) advertising, you pay only when someone clicks on your link from the search-engine results page or through a website that the PPC service fed your ad to. Google's AdWords and Yahoo's Publisher Network are the most well known PPC programs.

When you purchase your ad, you agree to pay a specific amount, from ten cents and up, each time your ad is clicked. While ten cents doesn't seem like much, consider that 100 clicks a day for 30 days is $300 a month. If your clicks aren't producing sales, that's money down the drain. The key to successful pay-per-click advertising includes:

Keywords. We have talked about the importance of keywords before, but nowhere else is it more important than in PPC advertising. While general keywords are okay in other advertising, in PPC ads you want to use highly targeted keywords. For example, if you sell riding boots, you don't want to buy the keyword "boots" because people looking for fashion boots or rain boots may see your ad and click on it.

Ad copy. Your ad should spell out what you offer in a way that is enticing to qualified customers, but not to people who can't or won't buy. And since you have only a few lines to get it right, you need to choose your words and your offer carefully.

Monitoring. The PPC services provide extensive tracking that will let you know how many times your ad has been shown, clicked on, from what keywords, and more. It will also tally what you've spent. Compare that to what you're making to ensure the ad is working.

Testing. Create several ads to test which has the best results.

Because PPC is effective but potentially risky, I recommend reading the *Ultimate Guide to Google AdWords* by Perry Marshall and Bryan Todd.

Podcasting/Internet Radio

According to a 2006 Arbitron Inc survey, over 30 million people listen to Internet radio on a weekly basis. iTunes reports having 100,000 podcasts in a variety of topics from big-name companies such as HBO and ESPN to smaller, home-based entrepreneurs. eMarketer predicted that by 2011, podcast advertising would grow to $400 million.

Internet radio and podcast popularity is growing for several reasons, including the ability to listen to what you want, when you want, and where you want. While many podcasts are done live, they are also recorded, so you can listen at 2 P.M. or 2 A.M. Further, radio podcasts can be downloaded onto your iPod or MP3 player or burned to a CD, allowing you to listen to radio shows and recordings while exercising or on the go.

Podcasting offers another way to show off your expertise, build credibility, and promote your business. Further, you can create more income streams by selling ad space, promoting affiliate products, and getting sponsors.

Podcasting or Internet radio involves recording a show and posting it online. While it may sound complicated, with today's technology it's quite simple. If you can plug a microphone into your computer, you can create a podcast. Most computers today come with basic audio-recording software.

Listen to podcasts or Internet radio shows before starting your own to get a feel for how they operate. You can visit iTunes, WSRadio. com or Blogtalkradio.com to find shows. To create your own show:

1. Decide on the type of show you want to produce. Will it provide information or entertainment? Will you have guests? Contests?

2. Develop a format. Most shows are divided into fifteen to twenty minute segments and usually have a guest.

3. Decide how often to produce a show. Many start out with a monthly show and increase it as they get comfortable. Regardless of how often you do your show, make sure you have enough content and can get the guests. This takes planning for weeks if not months in advance.

4. Gather your equipment. If you'll be interviewing people over the phone, you'll need a headset and a phone recorder that you can plug into your computer. Headsets are affordable and can be found at any office store. You can get a phone-recording controller at Radio Shack for about $30. You can use the audio-recording

software that came with your machine (e.g., Voice Recorder in Windows); however, for better recording quality and editing, you can get Audacity for free at *http://audacity.sourceforge.net*.

5. Develop your content and schedule interviews.

6. Find a place to host your podcast or Internet Radio show. If your website has the space and bandwidth, you can upload your podcast right to your web server. Or you can use audio storage services such as AudioGenerator.com or AudioAcrobat.com. There are many podcast hosting sites as well. Libysn.com and Podlot.com can host your site for free with some restrictions. Or you can host your show at WSRadio.com or Blogtalkradio.com.

7. Provide a variety of methods for listeners to access your recordings. Sometimes I like to listen online, and other times I want to download it. Give your listeners both options. What you want to avoid is forcing people to download your podcast if they don't want to.

8. Promote your podcast. Add it to your website, blog, and MySpace page. Promote it in your newsletter.

Plan for Work-at-Home Success

1. Send an e-mail to your list of friends to announce your new business.

2. Create a signature line for all e-mail and discussion group posts.

3. Join three discussion groups and one social networking site, and begin participating in discussions and sharing your ideas.

4. Submit your site to the major search engines.

5. Develop a newsletter or other item that allows you to collect names and e-mails from people who visit your site.

6. Send a press release announcing your new business to online PR services.

7. Choose three or four other online marketing strategies that you can do regularly.

CHAPTER TWENTY-THREE

Running a Successful Home-Based Business

BEING THE BOSS IS THE BEST POSITION TO BE IN. However, it's not for the faint of heart. As the boss, you're responsible for making sure all aspects of the business are running smoothly from accounting to customer service and advertising to collections. Wearing multiple hats requires organization, planning, and a can-do attitude.

Organization

Do you know what you have to do today? Who to call? Who to contact? What marketing tasks need to be done? Do you know where to find your materials? Organization is all about being able to sit down to work without wasting time figuring out what you need to do and looking for materials to do the job.

I'm not the best person to talk about organization, as I'm not very good at it. However, I know that good organization saves time and energy. I have also discovered that organizational styles vary from person to person. You may prefer to file by topic, while someone else will file alphabetically. The trick is to find the organizational system that works best for you. Some things to consider are:

- *Are your equipment and materials within reach?* Can you reach your reference books from your desk? Can you grab the page out of the printer without getting up?
- *Do you know what you need to do?* Is your calendar and to-do list readily available and easy to refer to as you work?
- *Do you have a place to put items you don't use all the time?*
- *File, don't pile.* I'm guilty of this. My file cabinet is right behind me, but I'm more likely to throw my filing in a box. Because I am a piler, I use bins to sort my filing. Each bin is for a specific file such as "receipts" or "paid bills." Other things you can try are to file at the end of the work period or hire someone (I hired my son) to do it for you.
- *Keep a list of what you need.* There's nothing worse than running out of printer ink in the middle of a big job. Tack a list on your bulletin board or wall where you can write down items you need such as ink, pens, staples, etc. That way, when you're ready to go get supplies you don't have to ransack your desk trying to determine what you don't have.
- *Keep phone numbers and other important information posted on your wall.* Even if you store contact information on your computer, have a list of frequently called numbers posted for times that your computer isn't on. Include any additional information such as customer numbers on the list as well. The only exception is bank account information and passwords. Don't post those.

Schedules

Most people believe they'll have more time when they eliminate the commute. And you will. But it won't be an abundance of time. A schedule is an important tool to make sure you get the work done and have more time for family or personal pursuits. Some tips for making your schedule include:

■ *Make your schedule as regular as possible.* This will keep you focused and help your family and customers respect your time.

■ *Start and end your day with routine.* Part of the fun of working at home is being able to mix things up. However, there's something to be said for routine. A routine makes it easier to get the day started and requires less mental energy, since you can work on auto-pilot. My day starts with putting the kids on the bus, getting coffee, turning on the laptop, checking e-mail, and going over my to-do list for the day. In the evening, I check my schedule for the next day, solidify my to-do list, check e-mail one final time, and then step away from the desk.

■ *Include breaks during the day.* Burning out is a sure-fire way to get off track. Avoid burnout by taking small breaks. Get coffee, take a short walk, play with the pet, or anything that gets you up and moving for a few minutes.

■ *Include everything, not just work activities, in your schedule.* If you don't add exercise to your schedule, it won't happen. Same with school activities, volunteering, getting the car fixed, or having lunch with friends.

E-mail management

E-mail can help with productivity or it can slow it down. Most people waste too much time checking and managing e-mail.

When I don't know what I should be working on, I check e-mail. And most of the time it's garbage. I delete approximately 90 percent of the e-mail I receive personally and professionally. Over the years, I have developed a few tips for making e-mail more manageable.

■ *Limit the number of e-mail accounts:* Having a separate personal and business account can separate personal from business-related e-mail, but having multiple personal and business accounts takes too much time to manage. Create additional e-mail accounts only if you absolutely need them as a method to keep organized.

■ *Limit the number of times you check e-mail each day:* Checking e-mail seems like a benign activity; yet checking e-mail is one of the biggest time wasters in a person's life. Check e-mail only two or three times a day. I check e-mail first thing in the morning, right before lunch, and when I'm getting ready to finish for the day. Do this for your personal accounts as well.

■ *Before giving your e-mail out, check to see what the recipient plans to do with it.* Will you be getting a newsletter? A free report? Is it a one-time e-mail or will you continue to receive e-mail from her?

■ *Keep a list of who you give your name and e-mail to:* Often people give out their name and e-mail, but then forget who they gave it to. I've had people get mad at me for sending a newsletter they asked for . . . twice. By keeping a list of the resources you have submitted your e-mail to, you can check when you get e-mails that you're not sure you asked for.

■ *Wash your e-mail:* If you download your e-mail, consider using a free program called Mail Washer (*www.mailwasher.net*) or use a web-based e-mail program to check your e-mail online first, deleting all the spam and e-mail that you're not going to read before you download it. This is a quick and easy method to delete e-mail you don't want, and keep just the e-mail you intend to read or respond to.

■ *Sort your e-mail:* One of the reasons that e-mail is so difficult to manage is that not all of it needs to be handled right away. Instead, it sits in the "In Box" and eventually gets lost in the sea of e-mail that came before and after it. The easiest way to manage e-mail is to develop a sorting process. Create folders for each of the e-zines or newsletters and other e-mails that you receive that require more time to read or are just simply information that you want to save. For example, I have e-mail folders for newsletters, receipts, affiliate-program details, and other important information I need to keep. Once the e-mail is sorted, set aside an hour or so each week to read your newsletters or items you have put off dealing with. Delete e-mails that you don't intend to ever look at again.

If you are overwhelmed by your e-mail, it may be time to unsubscribe from some newsletters or resources. Those that run their lists correctly will have an unsubscribe button at the bottom of the e-mail. Simply click the link to unsubscribe. If there is no link, check the e-mail for unsubscribe information. Usually an e-mail to the publisher asking to be removed from the list will work.

Managing the Workload

One of the biggest challenges to working at home is learning to pace yourself and only take on work that you can realistically manage. To ensure that you can meet all your deadlines:

■ *Know how much you can reasonably do well in a given period of time.* Track all tasks related to your work, including marketing, managing the business, and completing projects.
If it takes three hours to complete a project for one client, you'd want to think twice about taking on twenty clients in a week.

■ *Schedule your time to ensure your work gets adequate attention.*

■ *Organize your time and work area so you can work efficiently.*

■ *Use systems and automation whenever possible.* Don't send e-mails if an autoresponder can do it for you. Use automatic bill pay instead of writing checks.

■ *Know when to say no.* It can be hard to turn down work, especially if money is tight. But it will be worse for your business if you can't complete a project on time. Have a list of other professionals to whom you can refer overload work. Yes, you'll be giving away business, but you don't have time to do it anyway.

■ *Get help.* If you're in a bind, getting help to complete a project can be the difference between a happy, returning customer or a complaining one. If you need more time, ask the family to pitch in around the house so that you can dedicate more time to your business until the project is done. Create a list of freelancers that you trust who can help you complete work. Hire a virtual assistant to take care of management aspects of your business such as e-mail and phone calls.

Stay Motivated

Sometimes I'd rather do anything else (except clean the house) than work. Often it's because the project is no fun or overwhelming. But when you work for yourself, if you don't work, you don't get paid. So you need a bag of tricks to keep you motivated and focused when you'd rather take the day off. Here are my tricks:

- *Revisit your goals and dreams.* Sometimes a simple reminder about what you're working toward, whether it's to stay home with kids or to tell your boss to take a hike, can get you moving forward again.
- *Do the fastest, easiest thing on your list. Action creates momentum.* Sometimes by doing one thing, you create the energy you need to go on to do one more thing.
- *Listen to uplifting or energizing music.*
- *Take a nap.* This seems counterproductive, but a power nap can re-energize you. Just be careful that your short twenty- or thirty-minute nap doesn't turn into an all-day couch-potato fest.
- *Take a walk.* Getting out and moving can re-energize you as well as get your brain functioning. Some of my best ideas come to me while I'm out exercising. Consider bringing your cell phone or a tape recorder with you to store all these great ideas.

The above strategies are designed to deal with in-the-moment-doldrums that keep you from working. But there are other things you can do to ensure you have the energy and motivation to work, such as:

- *Pay attention to your peak work times and schedule your day to take advantage of them.*
- *Eat well, including energy-producing foods such as those with protein.* Avoid energy-draining sugary foods.

■ *Exercise.* Choose something fun like recreational soccer or a dance class. Even playing outside with the kids can get the heart rate up and boost morale.

■ *Get enough sleep.* Studies over the last few years suggest that a lack of sleep leads to more accidents and weight gain. It can also make it hard to focus and work.

■ *Don't become a work-at-home-aholic.* There is a very real chance that you'll end up working more hours than you do at your traditional job. This can lead to burnout, which can lead to business failure. Create and stick to your schedule. Take at least one, if not two, days off a week. Modify your schedule only in crunch situations. If you find that you're always in a crunch situation, reread the Managing the Workload section of this chapter.

■ *Have fun!* Your job may be dull and uninspiring, but working at home in a business or job of your choice gives you the opportunity to create something fulfilling and inspiring. Find ways to enjoy your work by choosing projects that sound interesting. Remember, it's not only about money. When you like what you do, you're in a better position to make more money.

Staying in the Game

When I was sixteen, I was like most teenagers who are eager and excited to get a driver's license. When I got it, I was agreeable to drive anywhere my parents wanted me to . . . for a while. Over time, the novelty of driving wore off. Today, I drive only when I have to.

Working at home can be the same way. There is a lot of excitement about putting things in place in anticipation of all the money that is going to come rolling in. But, eventually, the novelty wears off. This is especially true when things don't happen as quickly as you'd hoped and planned. Working at home is like the rest of life . . . stuff happens. And when stuff happens, sometimes you want to quit.

As you plan your work-at-home life you're probably saying, "That won't happen to me. I have what it takes." I hope that's true. But until you face the frustration and disappointment of not getting the results or money you had anticipated, you don't really know how difficult it can be to trudge on in the face of what seems like failure. I've quit various projects hundreds of times. Usually, I get back to them, finding the desire and energy to plod on. But it's not an easy task. To help you stay committed, no matter what:

- *Make a deal and seal it in writing.* Everyone has wishes and dreams, but most people let life steal them away. If you're truly committed to your goal, make a contract with yourself that outlines your goals and states that you won't ever give up. At the very least, give your effort a full twelve months before throwing in the towel.

- *Keep your eye on the prize.* I always say that a bad day working at home is better than a good day commuting to a job. But I have moments when I'm not so sure. Remembering why I work at home and reviewing my goals supply the motivation to keep going.

- *Do something related to your business every workday.* Doing something, even if it's a little thing, creates habit, which creates momentum to keep you moving forward.

- *Put things in perspective.* This is a challenge for me. I worry about everything. But, usually nothing is as bad as my mind can make it. To get perspective, step away from the project or event for a bit or get feedback from your mentor.

- *Evaluate your efforts and make a new plan.* If you're not getting results, take an honest look at all the activities you engage in to determine if you're focused on the important tasks or if something else isn't working. Readjust and refocus your efforts to get things back on track.

LAWS OF WORK-AT-HOME SUCCESS #㉙
Never, ever give up.

Growing and Expanding Your Business

Most people begin their work-at-home journey with one business project. Perhaps it will be a single product or service. To take your business to the next level, you'll need to expand on your foundation. To create a bigger market and expand your brand, consider:

- *Adding products.* Even if you provide a service, you can increase your profits by adding products. If you're a copywriter, you can sell information products (e-books) on copywriting. If your business is online, you can use affiliate or contextual-ad marketing to create more income from your website and/or blog.
- *Add services.* Make a list of additional services your customers need. If you're a copywriter, your customers may also need a desktop designer.
- *Expand your target market.* If you target moms, consider targeting dads or grandmas.
- *Expand your marketing efforts.* If you're primarily online, create an offline marketing campaign in your local area. If you're offline, build a website or blog.

Managing the Expansion

As your business grows, it will outgrow your ability to manage it as a one-woman show. You may have more requests for work than you can take on, or more projects than you can handle. This is good if you can manage the extra work. However, you're limited by time on how much work you can take, unless you also expand your manpower. To keep your business growing, consider:

- *Hiring help.* Hiring an assistant can free your time to focus on the money-making aspects of the business. Or hire others to provide your service or help manage orders. For example, if you have a writing business, you can take on freelance writers to complete work. You can continue to write as well, or simply manage the business and let the freelancers do the work.
- *Bring in a partner.* A partner can provide further capital, invest time, and bring new ideas. Choose a partner carefully and have a lawyer draw up a partnership plan.
- *Sell it.* This is an exit strategy, but selling your business can help it grow. In 1997, Julie Aigner-Clark invested her (and her husband's) money to create educational videos she named Baby Einstein. By 2000, the company was making $10 million a year. At that time, Julie sold a stake in the company to Artisan Entertainment and in 2001 sold the rest to Disney. Today, Baby Einstein includes toys and cartoons. Many other people have sold their businesses to larger companies and stayed on as a consultant. So selling doesn't mean you have to give up your business altogether.

Multiple Streams of Income

In 1993, Barbara Winter published a book called *Making a Living Without a Job*, in which she describes the concept of "multiple profit centers." When I read this book, I was intrigued. Instead of trying to make $5,000 a month from one business, I could make $1,000 a month from five businesses. Today, the idea of multiple income streams is popular, especially online. The benefits of operating several income streams include:

■ The ease of creating several smaller profit streams over one large profit stream.
■ Reduced risk. If one business tanks, the others can pick up the slack.
■ Keeping life interesting with something new always on the horizon.
■ Ease of capitalizing on your interests and talents.

However, developing multiple income streams has its problems, including:

■ Keeping track of everything that needs to be done with each income stream.
■ Giving enough attention to each profit center to make them profitable.
■ Start-up time for projects requires a lot of physical and mental energy and focus.

The best way to create multiple streams of income is to adhere to the basic tenets of this book, which include:

■ *Stick to what you know.* It's easier to make money from something you already know how to do.
■ *Keep your income streams related.* If you're a gardening expert, your income streams can include a landscaping business, information products on gardening or how to start a gardening business, and creating your own gardening tools.
■ *Don't start a new income stream until one is up and running.* This allows you to focus all your energy and time on getting

one business running, the systems in place to keep it going, and time to get the bugs out. Once you have it running, you can add another. But only one at a time.

■ *Be willing to let something go if it's not working, you don't like it, or you can't find the time for it.* Don't waste your time trying to work on a project that isn't profitable or that you don't enjoy, especially if you have other ventures that you like better.

Plan for Work-at-Home Success

1. Develop a system to track your invoices and income owed to you.

2. Organize your office and your life.

3. Create a schedule and stick to it.

4. Learn to manage e-mail.

5. Pace yourself to manage your workload.

6. Find ways to motivate yourself when you don't want to work or you want to quit altogether.

7. Find ways to grow and expand your business.

8. Consider adding an additional income stream.

Telecommuting Information, Associations, and Resources

Telecommuting Information

- Flexible Resources *www.flexibleresources.com*
- General Services Agency: Interagency Telework/ Telecommuting Site *www.telework.gov*
- Gil Gordon *www.gilgordon.com*
- June Langhoff's Telecommuting Resource Center *www.junelanghoff.com*
- Network World *www.networkworld.com/topics/telework .html*
- Oregon Office of Energy Telework Site *http://egov.oregon .gov/ENERGY/TRANS/Telework/telehm.shtml*
- Some Common—and not so Common Telecommuting Questions *www.jala.com*
- Telecommute Connecticut *www.telecommutect.com*
- Telework (Telecommuting) Benefits . . . and some issues *www.eto.org.uk/faq/faq03.htm*

- Work-at-Home Success *www.workathomesuccess.com*
- Work Options *www.workoptions.com*

Companies That Accept Applications for Contract Workers

Administrative Support/Virtual Assistants/Typing/Data Entry/Transcription

- Alderson Reporting *www.aldersonreporting.com*
- Axion Data *www.axiondata.com/employreq.htm*
- Connect Plus LCC *www.connect-dataplus.com/employ.shtml*
- CyberDictate *www.cyberdictate.com/company/employment*
- ExecuScribe *www.execuscribe.com*
- Mass Transcription *www.masstranscription.com/employment.php*
- Net Transcripts *www.nettranscripts.com/employment.htm*
- SpeakWrite *http://typist.youdictate.com/TypistNav/employment.htm*
- Transcription Studio *www.transcriptionstudio.com/transcribers.htm*
- Ubiqus Reporting *www.ubiqus.com*
- Virtual Office Temps *www.virtualassistantjobs.com/duties.html*
- VITAC Real Time Captioning *www.vitac.com/careers.htm*
- Working Solutions *www.workingsol.com/agents_page*

Accounting/Bookkeeping

- Bookminders (need to live in S. PA) *www.bookminders.com/careers/index.html*

Communities Guides

- About.com *http://beaguide.about.com*
- Bella Online *www.bellaonline.com/misc/joinus/index.asp*

Customer Service/Teleservices

- Access Marketing Corporation *www.axsmktg.com*
- Affina *http://affinahomeagent.com*
- ARO Business Process Outsourcing *www.callcenteroptions .com/careers.asp*
- LiveOps *www.liveops.com/become-agent/index.html*
- Voice Log *www.voicelog.com/careers.html*

Disabled Employees

- Lift, Inc. *www.lift-inc.org/apply.html*

Legal Transcription

- CyberDictate *www.cyberdictate.com/company/employment*
- Mass Transcription *www.masstranscription.com/ employment.php*
- Neal R. Gross *www.nealrgross.com/employment.htm*
- TypeWrite *www.typewp.com/9786.html*

Medical Transcription and Coding

- American Transcription Solutions *http://atsi-inc.com/ Careers.asp*
- ExecuScribe *www.execuscribe.com*
- LexiCode *www.lexicode.com/remoteathome.html*
- MD-IT *www.md-it.com/employment.htm*
- NJPR *www.njpr.com/employment.html*
- Outsourcing Solutions, Inc. *www.ositranscription.com/ recruiting.html*
- Presynct Technologies, Inc. *www.presynct.com/careers.html*
- Skilled Transcription Services *www.stsexperience.com*
- Spheris *www.spheris.com/careers*
- TransHealth *www.transhealth.com/employment.htm*
- United Medical Transcription *www.unitedtr.com*

Research Jobs

- Clicknwork *www.clicknwork.com/opportunities*

Translation and Interpretation Services

- Accurapid Translation *http://accurapid.com/accurapid/xlatorfr.html*
- Bilingva *www.bilingva.com/careers.html*
- Dialog One *www.dialog-one.com/opportunities.html*
- Ubiqus Reporting *www.ubiqus.com*

Tutoring and Teaching

- Aim For A Tutoring *www.aim4a.com/tutors.php*
- EduWizards *http://eduwizards.com/index.php*
- Electronic Classroom of Tomorrow *www.ecotohio.org/home.php?section-careers*
- Global Scholar *www.globalscholar.com*
- Growing Stars *www.growingstars.com/growingstars/tutorenquiry.jsp*
- Smart Thinking *www.smarthinking.com/static/e-structors/positions*

Writing

- Clicknwork *www.clicknwork.com/opportunities*
- Curriculum Content *http://curriculumcontent.com/about_us_career.html*
- CyberEdit *www.cyberedit.com/hub/jobs.shtml*
- FabJob.com *www.fabjob.com/jobs.html*

Telecommuting Job Search Websites

These are sites specifically designed to list current work-at-home job announcements. Some of these sites charge for their list of work-at-home jobs. They have been marked with a $ sign. Please remember that scammers will post their "jobs" on any site they can, so review Chapter 2 on avoiding scams to protect yourself.

- 2Work-At-Home.com *www.2work-at-home.com*
- HomeJobStop $ *www.homejobstop.com*
- Rat Race Rebellion *www.ratracerebellion.com*
- SOHO Jobs – Free and ($) *www.freesohojobs.com*
- Telecommuting Job Opportunities $ *www.tjobs.com*
- VirtualAssistants.com $ *www.virtualassistants.com*
- WAHM *www.wahm.com/jobs.html*
- Work-at-Home Success *www.workathomesuccess.com*

Freelance Job Resources—General Work

- Elance ($) *www.elance.com*
- Guru *www.guru.com*
- HomeworkersNet *www.homeworkersnet.com/jobs.html*
- Workaholics4Hire *www.workaholics4hire.com/main.htm*

Freelance Job Resources—Computer and IT Work

- Computer Jobs *www.computerjobs.com/homepage.aspx*
- Contract Job Hunter *www.cjhunter.com*
- Dice *www.dice.com/*
- Job Warehouse *www.jobwarehouse.com/jwc/search.cfm*
- JustTechJobs *www.justtechjobs.com*
- Planet Recruit *www.planetrecruit.com/channel/int*
- Project Spring *www.projectspring.com/freelance/index.html*
- Rent a Coder *www.rentacoder.com/RentACoder/default.asp*

Freelance Job Resources—Writing Work

- Absolute Write *www.absolutewrite.com/Markets.htm*
- Freelance Writing *www.freelancewriting.com/freelance-writing-jobs.php*
- MediaBistro *www.mediabistro.com*
- MTjobs *www.mtjobs.com*
- ProBlogger *http://jobs.problogger.net*

- Sun Oasis Jobs *www.sunoasis.com*
- WritersWeekly.com *www.writersweekly.com*

General Job Search Websites

These sites offer general job announcements. Once you access the website, use keywords such as "telecommute" and "work at home" to search the databases. See Chapter 7 for information on job searching using the Internet.

United States Job Search Websites

- 6 Figure Jobs *www.6figurejobs.com*
- AdQuest3-D *www.adquest3d.com*
- CareerBuilder Network *www.careerbuilder.com*
- Career Journal from the Wall Street Journal *www.careerjournal.com*
- Employment911 *www.employment911.com*
- Flipdog *www.flipdog.com*
- Job Central *www.jobcentral.com*
- Job.com *www.job.com/my.job*
- JobHunt *www.job-hunt.org*
- Jobs.com *www.jobs.com*
- KellyCareerNetwork *http://jobsearch.kellycareernetwork.com*
- Monster.com *www.monster.com*
- Net-Temps *www.net-temps.com*
- Portfolio *www.portfolios.com*
- True Careers *www.truecareers.com*
- WorkTree.com $ *www.worktree.com*
- Yahoo HotJobs *www.hotjobs.com*

Regional Northeast Job Search Websites

- Boston Job Bank *www.bostonjobs.com*
- Boston Works *http://bostonworks.boston.com*

- Find It Online *www.finditonline.com/sp?skin-0&aff-1*
- New Jersey Online *www.nj.com/jobs*
- Philadelphia Job-Circle *www.jobcircle.com*
- TriState Jobs *www.tristatejobs.com*

Regional Midwest Job Search Websites

- Career Board *www.careerboard.com*
- Minnesota Jobs *www.minnesotajobs.com*
- Online Columbia *www.onlinecolumbia.com/jobsearch.asp*

Regional South and Southeast Job Search Websites

- Florida Career Link *www.floridacareerlink.com*
- Triangle Jobs *http://jobs.triangle.com*
- Virginia Employment Commission *www.alex.vec.state.va.us*

Regional West Job Search Websites

- Alaska Job Center *www.ilovealaska.com/alaskajobs*
- Bay Area Jobs *www.bajobs.com*
- Colorado Jobs *www.coloradojobs.com*
- Oregon Employment Department *www.emp.state.or.us/empmtsvcs*
- Work Source Washington *www.wa.gov/esd/employment.html*

Home Business Resources

Affiliate Program Resources

- Affiliate Master's Course *http://aff-masters.sitesell.com/ internetincome.html*
- Affiliates Directory *www.affiliatesdirectory.com*
- Associate Programs *www.associateprograms.com*
- Clickbank *www.clickbank.com*
- Commission Junction *www.commissionjunction.com*
- Link Share *www.linkshare.com*
- Refer-It *www.refer-it.com*

Article Marketing Services, Directories, and Announcement Groups

- Article Announce Group at Yahoo *http://tech.groups .yahoo.com/group/article_announce*
- Article Announcement General Interest at Yahoo *http:// groups.yahoo.com/group/aageneral*

- Article Marketer *www.articlemarketer.com*
- Best Syndication *www.bestsyndication.com*
- Free Content at Yahoo Groups *http://finance.groups.yahoo .com/group/Free-Content*
- Free Reprint Articles at Yahoo Groups *http://groups.yahoo .com/group/Free-Reprint-Articles*
- ISnare *www.isnare.com*
- LadyPens *www.ladypens.com*

Autoresponder Services

- AWeber *www.aweber.com*
- Constant Contact *www.constantcontact.com*
- Get Response *www.getresponse.com*

Blog Services

- Blogger *www.blogger.com*
- Pingomatic *www.pingomatic.com*
- Technorati *www.technorati.com*
- Wordpress *www.wordpress.com*
- Wordpress *www.wordpress.net*

Business Information and Support

- Online Women's Business Center *www.sba.gov/aboutsba/ sbaprograms/onlinewbc/index.html*
- Small Business Administration *www.sba.gov*
- SCORE *www.score.org*

Coaching/Consulting Support Services

- Ether *www.ether.com* (Ether provides a phone number and will bill your clients.)

Contextual Advertising (PPC Advertising or Ad Feeds for Revenue)

- Google AdSense *www.google.com* (click on "Advertising Programs")
- Kanoodle *www.kanoodle.com/*
- Miva *www.miva.com/us/content/advertiser/overview.asp*
- Yahoo's Publisher Network *http://publisher.yahoo.com*

Direct Sales/MLM

- Direct Sales Tools *www.directsalestools.com*
- Direct Selling Association *www.dsa.org*
- Direct Selling University *www.directsellersuniversity.com*
- Direct Selling Woman's Alliance *www.mydswa.org*

Domain Registrars

- Godaddy.com *www.Godaddy.com*
- Register.com *www.register.com*

eBay and eBay Services

- Boutique Bargains *www.boutiquebargains.com*
- eBay *www.ebay.com*
- eBay Marketplace Research *http://pages.ebay.com/marketplace_research*
- Terapeak *www.terapeak.com*

E-mail Services

- Gmail *http://gmail.google.com* (Free e-mail account)
- MailWasher *www.mailwasher.com* (Wash e-mail before downloading)
- Yahoo Mail *www.yahoo.com* (Free e-mail account)
- You Send It *www.yousendit.com* (Send large files by e-mail)

Fax Services

- eFax *www.efax.com*
- Fax Digits *www.faxdigits.com*
- Fax Zero *http://faxzero.com*

Financing Resources

- Online Women's Business Center *www.sba.gov/aboutsba/sbaprograms/onlinewbc/index.html*
- Vfinance Venture Capital *www.vfinance.com*

Freelancer Sources

- Elance *www.elance.com*
- Guru *www.guru.com*
- Rent-a-coder *www.rentacoder.com* (Provides website help)

Information Product Creation

- Adobe Acrobat *www.adobe.com* (Software to create PDF documents)
- Lulu *www.lulu.com/en/products* (Create materials in a variety of formats)
- PDF995 *www.pdf995.com* (Free PDF software)

Intellectual Property Protection

- U.S. Patent and Trademark Office *www.uspto.gov*
- U.S. Copyright Office *www.copyright.gov*
- Legalzoom *www.legalzoom.com*
- Thomson Trademark Research *www.trademark.com/newsite2/index.html*

Internet Marketing Information

- Internet Based Moms *http://internetbasedmoms.com*
- Internetprofitplanning.com *www.InternetProfitPlanning.com*

Keyword Selection Tools

■ AdWordAnalyzer *www.adwordanalyzer.com*

■ Good Key Words *www.goodkeywords.com*

■ Google's Keyword Tool *https://adwords.google.com/select/KeywordToolExternal*

■ Wordtracker *www.wordtracker.com*

Merchant Account/Payment Processing

■ Authorize.Net *www.authorize.net*

■ Clickbank *www.clickbank.com*

■ Paypal *www.paypal.com*

Networking/Mastermind/Mentorship Groups

■ Internet Based Moms *www.internetbasedmoms.com*

■ Meet-Up *www.meetup.com* (Search your local area for work-at-home groups.)

■ Mom Masterminds *www.mommasterminds.com*

Press Release Distribution

■ PRNuke *www.prnuke.com*

■ USPRwire *www.usprwire.com*

■ PRFree *www.prfree.com*

■ PRLeap *www.prleap.com*

■ PRWeb *www.prweb.com*

■ PRZoom *www.przoom.com*

Public Speaking

■ American Training and Seminar Association *www.americantsa.com*

■ National Speaker's Association *www.nsaspeaker.org*

■ Public Speaking Tips *www.speaking-tips.com*

■ Speaker Match *www.speakermatch.com*

■ Toastmasters International *www.toastmasters.org*

Publicity

- Expert Click *www.expertclick.com*
- PR Leads *www.prleads.com* (Journalists use this service to find experts to interview for articles.)

Search Engines and Directories

- AltaVista: *http://addurl.altavista.com/addurl/new*
- Google *www.google.com*
- MSN *http://search.msn.com/docs/submit.aspx*
- Open Directory *www.dmoz.org/add.html* (Other engines and directories such as AOL and Yahoo use Open Directory's data to list on their resources.)
- Scrub the Web *www.scrubtheweb.com/addurl.html*
- Yahoo *https://siteexplorer.search.yahoo.com/submit*

Social Networking

- Facebook *www.facebook.com*
- Linked In *www.linkedin.com*
- MySpace *www.myspace.com*
- Ryze *www.ryze.com*

Teleconferencing Line

- Free Conference *www.freeconference.com*
- Free Conference Call *www.freeconferencecall.com*

Virtual Assistant Resources and Information

- AssistU *www.assistu.com*
- International Virtual Assistants Association *www.ivaa.org*
- Staff Centrix *www.msvas.com*
- Virtual Assistant Certification *www.vacertification.com*

Voice Mail (free)

- eVoice *www.evoice.com*
- Simple Voicebox *www.simplevoicebox.com*

Web Hosting Resources

- Compare Webhosts *www.comparewebhosts.com*
- Tophosts *www.tophosts.com*

Web Hosting Services

- Host Gator *www.hostgator.com*
- MomWebs Hosting *www.momwebs.com*
- PowWeb *www.powweb.com*
- Web.com *www.web.com*

Work-at-Home Information

- 2Work-At-Home *www.2work-at-home.com*
- Bizymoms *www.bizymoms.com*
- Entrepreneur.com *www.entrepreneur.com*
- Home-Based Working Moms *www.hbwm.com*
- Home Biz Women *www.homebizwomen.com*
- WAHM.com *www.wahm.com*
- Webmomz.com *www.webmomz.com*
- Work at Home Community *www.workathomecommunity.com*
- Work-at-Home Success *www.workathomesuccess.com*

Business Research Resources

- Forbes Digital Tool *www.forbes.com*
- Hoover's Online *www.hoovers.com*
- Media Fortune Magazine *www.fortune.com*
- U.S. Securities and Exchange Commission *www.sec.gov*
- Vault Reports Inc. *www.vaultreports.com*

Consumer Protection Resources

- Better Business Bureau *www.bbb.org* (You can locate local BBBs, get advice, check out a company, and more.)
- Better Business Bureau Online *www.bbbonline.org*
- Federal Trade Commission *www.ftc.gov/bcp/consumer.shtm*
- Internet Scam Busters *www.scambusters.org*
- Work-At-Home Scam Prevention *www.workathomescam prevention.com*

Online Education and Learning Centers

ALLEN LEIGH'S DISTANCE LEARNING ONLINE COURSE IN WEB DESIGN

- Classes USA *www.classesusa.com*
- Colorado Technical University Online *www.ctuonline.edu*
- Ed Surf Online Distance Learning *www.edsurf.net*
- Free Education Net *www.free-ed.net*
- Free Skills *www.freeskills.com*
- New Mexico Tech Computer Center Free User Classes *www.nmt.edu/tcc/classes/homepage.html*
- Strayer University *www.strayer.edu*
- ThirdAge.com *www.thirdage.com/learning*
- University Alliance Online *www.universityalliance.com*
- University of Phoenix *www.phoenix.edu*
- World Wide Learn *www.worldwidelearn.com*

Index